Power Play

*Taming the Work Circus
From the Inside Out*

DR. BRIDGET COOPER

ISBN-13: 978-0692669273
ISBN-10: 0692669272

DEDICATION

This book is dedicated to my daughters, Jessica and Elena.
May you embrace your personal power,
rise proudly to the challenges life brings you,
and never settle for anything less than
the extraordinary, abundant, glorious life you so deserve.

CONTENTS

TRIBUTES

"Believe you can and you're halfway there."
~ Theodore Roosevelt

When you're writing a book, there are countless people who touch the process and leave their fingerprint on it. I know I'm leaving people out before I begin, so I'll start off by thanking the Universe for everyone and everything that didn't make it onto this list. I appreciate every story, every adversity, and every example you've offered that has made its way into my consciousness and, therefore, into this book. Though we often forget in the hectic and unconscious nature that is our lives, we affect one another in small and large ways in each passing moment.

Most importantly, to my astonishing, beautiful, and bright daughters, Jessica & Elena: Everything I do, I do in the hopes of making this world a better place so that you can share in its abundance. Thank you for challenging me by your very existence to manifest that while still putting our life together front and center. I am blessed to be your mommy and will work tirelessly and joyfully to show you how amazing life can be, even in the toughest and darkest of places.

To Lisa: We have had countless conversations about work and life and the circus that plagues both arenas, and us personally. You've encouraged me to bring my message to the masses and I'm forever in your debt. What would I do without the promise you've made to join me on the road someday? My sixth book, with you as my co-author, is going to be the best yet! Anything else on your bucket list that we can tackle together? We are loving warriors of this thing called "life" and I'm blessed to call you my friend.

To Auntie Joanie: I've been blessed to have had you in my world since I came into it. You've been a bright light of love, encouragement, and joy for me, guiding me out of some shadowy places. As your shadow, what could be more poignant for me? ☺ Thank you for editing this manuscript and for all of your love and support along my journey. You are so loved and appreciated.

To Kim S.: Thank you for being one of my biggest cheerleaders and encouraging me every step of the way. We are on this journey together and I hope that you see the promise you hold for this world woven in the pages of this book.

To Kim M.: I'm so grateful for your wit, your wisdom, and your heart. You've offered plenty of grist for this mill and an abundance of support along my journey. I'll be forever thankful for Mulch Day and your trust.

To Kimberlea & Marianne: You swooped in late in the process as my accountability partners but you've been key to the completion of this labor of love. I'm so glad to share my journey with you!

To Kelly, my amazing cover designer: Thank you for continuing to up your game and for bringing your natural talents to each new book cover. I deeply appreciate your keen eye and rare ability to see what I cannot adequately describe. You take my imagination and make it a reality and I cannot thank you enough!

To Tania, my talented photographer: Thank you for your sense of humor, style, composition, and lighting. Your keen eye, gentle presence, and love for your craft made the photo a joy (and a blast) to pose for. Okay, so the bull whip as a prop didn't hurt!

To Thom: I had to write this book just so I could have you write my foreword! Thank you for your careful, considerate, and inventive take on this book. I've thoroughly enjoyed our conversations, meetings, and partnerships along the way and look forward to many more.

To the colleagues and clients I've been blessed to guide over the years: Your challenges have challenged me, and in so doing, given me the incentive to help others through sharing our the ups and downs of this circus we call "work." I've witnessed you coming into your personal power, taking up your space in your chair, and so many people have benefited as a result. Thank you for trusting me to assist you in transforming your businesses and your approach to life.

To my advance reviewers: Thank you for taking the time and energy to read my manuscript and share your thoughts and suggestions! You've made this a better book and I'm forever grateful.

To my cadre of supporters near and far: I'm so grateful to have you cheering for me as I've hit the potholes inherent in any journey. I know I didn't name each of you separately here, but please know how much gratitude I have for your appearance on my path. We can't get through this thing called "life" alone so I thank you for helping to get me through.

To whoever has/had possession of my original draft of this book after I accidentally left it behind on a plane in November: Thank you for placing this challenge in my path so that I could know that I am capable of starting over and prevailing in spite of the loss. May my words bring you guidance, insight, and awareness.

To the adversaries and bullhooks I've been injured by in my own circus: Thank you for embodying the toxic and complementary qualities of carelessness and forcefulness because, as a result, you've given me the opportunity to demonstrate my true grit. I continue to pray that you'll transform your pain into a power that serves you and the world.

To you, the reader: Thank you for being brave enough to pick up this book and challenge yourself to take charge of your destiny. With enough of you out there owning your personal power, we can change the world, bringing success, abundance, and freedom to everyone willing to join us. Let's sprinkle that stuff everywhere!

"There will always be people in your life who treat you wrong.
Be sure to thank them for making you strong." ~ Zig Ziglar

FOREWORD

.

"Great minds discuss ideas. Average minds discuss events.
Small minds discuss people." ~ Eleanor Roosevelt

In the business world - as executives, entrepreneurs, managers, and team members - we are immersed in visions of productivity, progress, accomplishment, growth, confidence, and recurring success. All are wonderful virtues that we strive to embrace. But few organizations operate at these high levels of synchronous euphoric bliss. Rather, they experience the more common themes of stress, drama, doubt, bias, negativity, and pressure. Employees feel isolated and powerless to improve their surroundings and the organization morphs into a beleaguered culture in a seemingly uncontrollable tailspin.

Enter Dr. Bridget Cooper – the remover of limits, the restorer of choice and champion of those who seek the recipe for a positive and productive life. As a personal friend and valued business associate, I know her to be a skilled professional who shares her knowledge, expertise and inspiration to the benefit of all who take her wisdom to heart.

In this, Dr. Cooper's fourth book, she investigates how stress, drama, and isolation in organizations create problems with individuals and among teams that lead to tragic consequences. Most people are comfortable being victims, even though they *can* choose not to be. Dr. Cooper explains why avoiding stress, drama, and isolation are just choices. It's just a decision; a big one that requires a personal commitment to yourself, and needs a roadmap to follow, but you *can* define yourself! You may be, as Bridget says, "at the mercy of a multitude of other factors, but you can influence those factors!"

I have personally seen what happens to a highly effective organization when a 'professional victim' infiltrates a team. But I've also witnessed the power of a team pulling together to take control, make better choices, regain the energy and culture that makes them productive. I've seen positive people drive away the stain that would otherwise destroy the joy, productivity, harmony, and enormous sense of accomplishment that a high-performance organization can experience.

Getting to that point, regaining that posture as an organization, is what Dr. Cooper's work is all about. She will give you the tools, the thought shifts, the light at the end of the tunnel, and the power to "excuse yourself from the circus that engulfs you."

So, if you'd like to discover, or *recover*, your personal power, and be the master your own life story … read on.

Thom Stimpel
Business Advisor & Managing Director
Proactive Business Improvements, LLC

"Most of the shadows of life are caused by
standing in our own sunshine." ~ Ralph Waldo Emerson

Do It Anyway
Credited to Mother Teresa

People are often unreasonable,
illogical and self-centered;
Forgive them anyway.

If you are kind,
people may accuse you of selfish ulterior motives;
Be kind anyway.

If you are successful,
you will win some false friends and true enemies;
Succeed anyway.

If you are honest and frank,
people may cheat you;
Be honest anyway.

What you spend years building,
someone could destroy overnight;
Build anyway.

If you find serenity and happiness,
they may be jealous;
Be happy anyway.

The good you do today,
people will often forget tomorrow;
Do good anyway.

Give the world the best you have,
and it may never be enough;
Give the world the best you've got anyway.

You see, in the final analysis,
it is between you and God [your higher power];
It was never between you and them anyway.

1

PROLOGUE

"It's not the load that breaks you down.
It's the way that you carry it." ~ Lou Holtz

If all the world's a stage, all the work's a circus.

We've been taught to believe that we are the masters of our own destinies but we constantly feel confined by the sideshow that dominates most of our waking hours. What does this sideshow encompass? Stress, drama, and isolation. Those three factors, my friend, are at the root of all organizational culture problems. How does this play out in the workplace? People feel:

- Overwhelmed
- Distrusting
- Disconnected

It's no small wonder that we feel all of these things. It's tough out there. The majority of people who are working in organizations are miserable at some level. We are stressed out, exhausted, and feeling unappreciated. There always seems to be more work than there are hours in a day. We spend most of our waking hours on the job (or accessible to it) so it becomes the center of our existence. When we aren't at the office, we're still glued to our mobile devices, ready to pounce on the next email, update, text, or phone call. Our lives are rotating around what's urgent, while we may have lost complete track of what's important. We are experiencing task and information overload.

Employees are continually challenged to work *harder*, but we are missing the keys to working *smarter*.

It's no small wonder that we feel overwhelmed, like hamsters on a wheel that just keeps getting faster and faster. We don't how to get off so we just keep going, hoping for relief at some distant point in the future. Some of us have even given up hope that it'll ever be different. We've thrown in the towel and submitted to our beleaguered existence. Whether we want to face it or not, we've handed over our power and become the victim in our own life story. We're behind bars and we don't recognize that we are holding the key.

This would be tragic on its own, but it's far bigger than that. There are so many people who are existing like this, to one degree or another, and the collective victimhood has tragic consequences for corporations, organizations, and communities. Instead of being in charge of our destiny, we are taking a backseat and watching as "the world" takes over.

We have all sorts of reasons as to why this makes sense. Our narrative is all about "them" and "it" and how the "others" make things so in our reality. If only "they" would do something differently. When "they" change, everything will be better. If "it" would get its act together, things would improve for you. We are taught this in popular media, with our strict definition of good and evil. We are encouraged to find someone or something to blame, making the "other" the bad guy which of course makes us the good guy. Life, my friends, is always more complicated than that. I've been analyzing and assessing people, places, and things since before I could walk, and I assure you that even the most terrible of people have mothers who love them. In this next example you'll see what happens in an organization when someone buys into their victim stance.

Problem: Our product development cycle was long so we were always late to market and missed the beneficial early adopters.

To solve the problem, we built a great team, with amazing communication and commitment to the process, and delivered our first product in a record 241 days.

We had earned the attention of a lot of people in the company, some of whom wanted to tie their names to this project, even though they had nothing to do with our process, products or success. Lee was one of these people. Lee felt victimized by the circumstances s/he encountered in the business world, and was completely blind to the fact that the majority of the problem was a false sense of aptitude, made worse by a bad attitude, and fed by greed, impatience, and a nasty -and unjustified- superiority complex. S/he was skilled in the art of immediately pushing the wrong buttons, trying to influence decisions and circumstances far outside of assigned responsibilities, and generally putting people on the defensive in five minutes or less.

My team was able to fend off a great deal of the negativity in this person, but when I had to travel, I'd come back to a group with their heads full of poison, no energy, no morale, no continuity … all because Lee had "taken control." Unfortunately, so many people, including those in decision making roles, don't know how to deal with a Lee, so I did move on … and take my people … and build a new team … and Lee failed miserably in replacing us.

When you introduce a "professional victim" to even the strongest team, they will suck the energy, collaboration and commitment from your people faster than you can imagine!

So, does this story imply that there are *no* victims in life because Lee claimed victim status but wasn't? Of course there are. People victimize other people all of the time. We have seen this in small and large scale and to greater and lesser degrees. Why? Because that's what people, especially injured, inattentive, broken people *do*. When we feel small, we often give into a basic need to press others beneath us, somehow, some way. This sounds like terrible news if your brain stops at this intersection, but you're way too smart for that. I'm inviting you to let the following statement wash over you.

You are only a victim for as long and as deeply as you want to define yourself as such.

There are some of you who, at this very instant, are practically yelling at this book. "What do you know about my experience? I have a right to feel like a victim!" Well, of course you do. When a person (or the world) does bad things to us it's valid to feel injured and wronged. It's appropriate to feel indignant, even furious. For a time. Then it's decision time. You get to decide how long you'd like to hold onto that victim badge. You can choose if you'd like to be defined as the victim in your life story, or the hero. Being victimized and living as a victim are very different things. One is tied to a circumstance or event; the other is a way of life. You can, in fact, be victimized and not remain the victim.

Am I making it sound too easy? In a way, it kind of *is* that easy. It's a decision, that starts with a recognition, one that is easy to sweep under the proverbial rug: We only get to live this life once, and the time we have here isn't unlimited and our end is usually not in our direct control. Sure, you could pitch yourself off a bridge and remove the mystery, but short of you making your own end, you're at the mercy of a multitude of other factors. Most of these factors are under your influence (healthy habits, safe driving, etc.), but most are not under your control (genetics, actions of others).

What *is* under your control is how you <u>think</u> about your life, how you <u>feel</u> about your circumstances, and what you <u>do</u> with the resources you *do* have.

You have the power.

You can think, feel, and act like a victim for as long as it serves your grief process, for as long as you need to reconcile what happened and how you got there. Maybe learn a little from the experience? At some point, you get to decide if you want this occurrence (or some series of occurrences) to *define* you; if you want them to build how you think about yourself and the world. That, folks, is entirely in your control.

Power is seen by some as a dirty word. For those of us who have been violated by those holding more power than we did, it's a provocative topic. Countless people in places of power have violated their positions and hurt those who depended on them. We rail against power. In my work with individuals and organizations, I'm outspoken about the importance of being in power. I get reactions that run the gamut, but a large number of people get suspicious of my intentions, like I'm suggesting an overthrow of some sort.

I admit it. I am. I'm absolutely advising an overthrow of the most magnificent variety: Of *you*. Of your personal power. Your dominion over you. Not over others: Over *you*.

Take back your power.

Sometimes, okay, **often**, this means running against the tide of public opinion. There is an abundance of people out there who are wedded to feeling done unto and don't take too kindly to the message of true empowerment. Don't be fooled by their social media posts: Those posts package far better than the truth, the truth that they don't know the road out of their dead-end lives. They are stuck in façade-ville and if you speak up about becoming the hero in your life story it will threaten them in their "comfort." Take it from personal experience, depending on how gently or boldly you take on this new worldview, you may lose people. In the same way that you were attracted to them in the first place because you shared some of the same thinking, when you start seeing the *world* differently, you will see *one another* differently. They may jump on board, happy that you crossed paths and your hero-stance is their new inspiration to take charge of their lives. Or, they might think, simply put, that you're a giant pain in the ass.

> "You are as big as your enemies
> and as small as your fear." ~ Anonymous

As with everything, you have a choice to make: Their opinion or yours? I know you know this already but it bears repeating right here: They don't have to live your life, only you get to do that. The ball is in your court to make decisions that make sense for you, and those decisions may include letting go of people who are stuck in victim mode. Until you've reconciled that possible reality, you might just float between the shores, not choosing the past *or* the future.

What does this all have to do with your experience at work? Absolutely everything.

The problems we face at work — especially the personal and interpersonal ones — can often make us feel like we are in captivity. We are captive to our jobs, our responsibilities, our debt, our self-image. I can't tell you how many people have told me that they are miserable at work but "can't leave." They cite a host of factors (tough marketplace, good benefits, too old to start over) for staying, so they suffer on.

If you're an executive and these employees are miserable, but they are staying, why should you care? Why does it matter if they are miserable if they are doing their jobs?

Because, they aren't doing their best job.

How do I know? I know this just like you know this. You know that when you are doing something and you're miserable, you're not doing your best.

I've identified three main symptoms that show that you're working in a circus of sorts which I've nicknamed the "triple threat." They are:

Stress

Drama

Isolation

When these elements take hold of a culture, they literally suck the energy, positivity, and productivity right out of it. They are there, wreaking havoc on your company, but trying to dig into them draws you into their vortex. Problems enter but never escape, they just get bigger and draw more and more things into their essence. You want to reduce them, but they just seem to get bigger and bigger and take more and more resources into them. They are freedom killers. Destroyers of all good things, of everything you've worked so hard to build and that you fight to protect. But the more you fight them, the bigger they seem to become because they've taken on a force of their own. They've locked you in and thrown away the key.

"Sometimes I can't figure out if I'm at preschool or at a high school. Oh, wait. I'm at work." ~ Anonymous

So, how do you tame this circus and break free from the chains? I wouldn't pose the problems if I was going to leave you hanging, silly. Read on.

This book guides you in two ways:

1. Staying away from the **triple threat** (stress, drama, & isolation) before your freedom is taken from you.
2. Getting you out of captivity once you've been drawn in.

When I was forming this book, I wanted to make certain that I had a strong message, a valiant purpose. So, I asked myself a question I ask all of my clients:

If I had a magic wand, where would I aim it?

There is unrest in the world coming from so many directions, seemingly all at once. We are searching for relief, for answers, for accountability. My purpose is to alleviate as much suffering, both short- and long-term, as I can while I'm here. What is causing the pain? What is the source of the pain? I came up with four targets for my handy-dandy magic wand:

- The **victim stance,** wherein people not understanding their own **personal power.**
- Understanding where **stress** comes from and alleviating it.
- Finding ways to get their **needs met** healthfully so they can tame the drama.
- Recognizing the **brevity of our time** on this planet and making decisions about things accordingly.

"If your actions inspire others to dream more, learn more, do more, and become more, you are a leader." ~ John Quincy Adams

Companies have communication and courage deficits, with good reason. Lawsuits and workplace violence dominate the media, putting corporations in a fearful, defensive position. More and more often, they are stuck in a recursive "what if?" position: What if we are sued? What if he becomes violent? What if other employees don't like the outcome and morale suffers? What if we take action and the project gets delayed or derailed? So we sit on it. We hope it gets better. We take a little bit of action, but nothing decisive, nothing that communicates a standard of practice or expectation that will create a positive shift in culture.

By avoiding the tough issues and hiding behind lawyers and complicated processes, we are feeding the drama which increases problems on so many levels of workplace culture. We are teaching our employees that inappropriate, destructive, and manipulative behavior will be enabled and excused. The message is that problematic employees are provided loyalty, which diminishes the destructive experiences of those in their war path. The problem employee is afforded the luxury of special, forgiving treatment which has two critical outcomes:

1. The problem employee is permitted to continue wreaking havoc on the workplace.
2. The good employees who have been negatively affected by the problem employee are sent the strong message that inappropriate, ineffective behavior is tolerable and that *their experience doesn't merit working toward a solution.*

In effect, any company that chooses fear over courage in addressing problem employees is choosing to keep a poor employee and lose good employees, or at least "dumb down" the standard of work. Why would good people stay in a company like that? Or, why would they put in maximum effort for a company who hasn't done their due diligence to take care of them?

"Silence encourages the tormentor,
never the tormented." ~ Elie Wiesel

C-Level executives: This book was written with you in mind. I know you're at a loss when you see the paralyzing effects of this circus environment. You try to implement new measures to help employees feel less stressed and more invested in their work: Compressed work weeks, healthy lifestyle initiatives, work-from-home options, and so on. You try to remain competitive in the marketplace by producing more, better, and faster. Your healthcare costs skyrocket with employee claims (healthcare, disability), absenteeism, and turnover climbing and climbing. What are you doing wrong?

You're focusing on the symptoms, not the ailment. At the core of any virtually any issue that you face traces back to a cultural issue that is ripping apart the fabric of every challenged community, company, and family: A failure to understand and accept personal responsibility. It's not a blame game, it's a boundaries game. Underneath it all is the recognition of a two-part puzzle of **control** and **choice**. You've got to lead them to the realization that they always have choice and recognition of where they have control and how they can contribute to the circumstances that they find themselves in. In "empowerment" and "engagement" circles, you, my friend, have hit the motherload.

"Our greatest freedom is the freedom
to choose our attitude." ~ Victor Frankl

~ Circus Monkeys ~

I've been consulting with organizations for over a decade, tackling their toughest cultural issues. The problem is that my biography shares who many of these clients are so when I share stories, I have to protect their anonymity. Sometimes I shift the details so that identities are unidentifiable. Nevertheless, many of my professional stories can't be told because they would compromise my professional ethic of confidentiality.

I solicited stories from colleagues, friends, and clients so that you could connect to these concepts with real-life examples. Most are professional, some are personal, but all are powerful in illustrating the destruction these culture killers can levy onto an organization, starting at the individual level. After all, companies are made up of the people who work there, so if the people are unhealthy, so is the organization. As I always say, people don't hang up their crazy at the door, they bring it right into work with them.

For those that are about me personally, I can share my internal dialogue and humanity instead of the ringside seats I held to someone else's struggle. I'm a big believer that our personal struggles show up in our work and in our offices. Don't even get me started on the relationships we develop at work (platonic, romantic, and sexual) and how those can wreak havoc on stress, drama, and isolation levels.

How do you get these sorts of pickles to stay in their jar and not come into your world in the first place? I wish I had the fairy dust to sprinkle to make them completely avoidable, but I'm fresh out of it. We all fall into trouble at times, even those of us committed to steering clear of them altogether. Although I can't give you any magic potion, I can give you a few really useful pointers, and that's what this book is all about:

Giving you the tools and thought shifts to empower you to excuse yourself from the circus that engulfs you. Delivering your POWER PLAY.

As my mother used to say, "the one with more awareness has more responsibility." Armed with this book, you can welcome that awareness and claim more responsibility. Know another word for responsibility? *Power.* Want to own that for yourself? Ready to crack that whip and tame that circus? In the words of the insightful Bob Seger, turn the page....

"Imagine what 7 billion humans could accomplish if we all loved and respected each other." ~ A. D. Williams

2

TICKET TO THE BIG TOP

"You either learn to play hard ball or
you become the ball." ~ Crystal Woods

Like a lot of you, I've been working since I was a teenager.
I've been a clerk, waitress, telemarketer (gulp), maid, administrative
assistant, intern, bank teller, therapist, recruiter, instructor, speech
writer, manager, consultant, professor, coach, and held countless
volunteer positions, both as a leader and a lackey. I've seen my fair
share of problems, both big and small, that cut across status, gender,
experience, geography, and industry. My tendency to analyze people
and situations is equaled only by my inclination to bring relief to
them. So, over the three decades I've spent working, I've gathered a
lot of observations, insights, and thankfully for you, solutions to the
pains that we face trying to make a living.

A coach of mine, in an effort to determine my "market
dominating position," once asked me how my best client would
describe me. I knew immediately that he would say,

"Bridget makes me a better leader by being a better person first."

Shortly thereafter, when I was in a meeting with that very client and shared this assumption with him, he said that I took the words right out of his mouth. This was exactly how he'd describe the work that I do with people. Not bad. If I decide to change careers I might have a future as a psychic medium.

What does this cute story have to do with you and this book? Absolutely everything. I am here to create dynamic and powerful shifts in the way people relate to themselves and other people so that they can be abundant at home and at work and in their communities. I do this by enhancing their awareness of what is *really* going on when trouble strikes and therefore how they can effectively address it, and hopefully prevent or dilute it going forward. I offer some fast fixes and some slow cures. I give you the benefit of all the clatter in my head that plagues me when I see a problem and feel compelled to diagnose and treat it.

Truth be told, I don't want you stumbling around bumping into problems and challenges one more day. You'll have plenty of issues to contend with on this planet without struggling through those that have solutions! I'm offering you the solutions. It's up to you if you want to use them. I know that change is hard, and, in order to help cure what ails you, I'm going to invite you to change the way you think about certain things. My approach is simple:

The way you think about things creates…

The way you feel about things which creates…

The way you act upon things.

This, in turn, creates your experience.

In other words, if I can change your mind, I can, in fact, change your life.

So, wait! Am I saying that the circus you're experiencing at work that is created by stress, drama, and isolation is all IN YOUR HEAD? Absolutely not. What I am saying is that the way you approach situations (mentally, emotionally, and tactically) as well as the challenges posed by stress, drama, and isolation absolutely ARE governed by your head. And I'm here to change all of that gobbledygook that's clouding your vision of how to minimize all the trappings.

First, we need to talk about what's at the root of all conflict and disorder: Needs. The basic needs that we all have to have fulfilled in order to feel confident, safe, and satisfied. When they aren't fed, well…

~ Bring In The Big Top ~

The circus tends to get brought to town for one simple reason: People's needs aren't being met so, in response, they act out in dysfunctional ways. Let's review each of the four core needs one by one: *Control, Connection, Purpose*, and *Validation*.

Control. People like to be in control, often of circumstances, events, and other people. The world is a scary place on a host of levels and the more control we are able to have, the less fearful we become. Phrases like, "you got this" and "master of his domain" come from this assertion. When you're "large and in charge" you're touting the fact that you're in control. It feels good to be in control because the opposite is to be out of control and no one likes that.

Author's note: There are those of us out there, however, who are exploring the usefulness of intentionally letting go of control. The utility of that is in accepting things as they are (vs. how we want them to be) that we can reach the clarity to intentionally decide to use our power to control the right things instead of the impossible things. The need for control is real, yet the more we investigate it, it's more an illusion than a reality.

Connection: We are social beings. We crave connection with others to varying degrees. We want to be in relationships with others to our level of comfort (think, extrovert vs. introvert). Sometimes we connect in unhealthy ways just to serve the need to be connected.

Purpose: The pinnacle dilemma most people face over the course of their lives is answering the question: "Why am I here?" It's the traditional mid-life crisis conundrum. For employees, it's about having a reason for getting up every day, putting on your suit, and braving the stressors that work brings.

Validation: We like to feel like we matter, like we are valued, like we are appreciated. At work, so many people feel overlooked for their contributions and investments in the company, often only getting feedback from their leaders when things are going wrong (or at annual review time).

You can easily see how central these are to promoting effectiveness and commitment at work. When these needs aren't being met, they lead to conflict, dysfunction, and people resort to downright crazy tactics to get them met. In other words, when people aren't getting their needs met, work turns into a 3-ring circus.

How? The culture killers (stress, drama, and isolation) are caught up in this dysfunctional adaptation to not getting one or more of these core needs met. When people aren't getting their need(s) met for:

Control: They get anxious and/or angry and want to manage those feelings so they are likely to try to control things that may not be in their purview to control. They get overwhelmed and stressed out.

Connection: They may feel isolated or paranoid about what is happening and may do a variety of undermining things such as enclosing, creating drama, and being reactive/emotional.

Purpose: They are likely to slack off, not feeling invested in their work and may check out of the company altogether.

Validation: They are likely to stir up lots of drama and other attention-seeking behaviors in order to be noticed in some way, shape, or form.

How does this analysis help you to manage the culture killers? By heading them off at the pass. If you know that people require these basic needs to be met and you've got a situation brewing that is going to compromise that, you can be intentional about creating opportunities for those needs to be met. Need an example?

Let's suppose you know there's a reorganization coming to your company and you're going to be shuffling people vis a vis reporting relationships, groupings, and geographically in the building. You can anticipate that all four of the core needs are going to be shaken up:

- *Control,* because they won't be in it.

- *Connection,* because theirs will be shifting.

- *Purpose,* because they might be feeling disconnected from the "why" of the reorg ("what's the point of this?").

- *Validation,* because in the shuffle, you might forget to acknowledge the work they are doing and the strife that the reorg caused them.

If you can see those freight trains coming ahead of time you can prepare for and avoid them. What does this look like? Well, I don't want to spoil the revelations coming in later chapters, but here's a teaser. You can satisfy their need(s) for:

- *Control*, by letting them decide, communicate, implement, or be in charge of something (anything).

- *Connection*, by staying in close contact with them, checking in to see how they are doing, and really listening to their apprehensions and concerns. You might even sponsor events (luncheons, etc.) with employees to give them time to socialize.

- *Purpose*, by explaining how the change will help the business long-term and how their part in it will help to predict its success or failure.

- *Validation*, by empathizing with their position, telling them that if you were them you'd probably feel the same way and help guide them out of that from there.

"If you are willing to look at another person's behavior toward you as a reflection of the state of their relationship with themselves rather than a statement about your value as a person, then you will, over a period of time, cease to react at all." ~ Yogi Bhajan

~ What To Expect In This Book ~

In this book, you'll read about the culture killers that result in disappearing productivity, job satisfaction, and results: Stress, drama, and isolation. I'll offer stories to illustrate how these energy sucks take hold as well as what you can do to reduce their pull. If, by the end of the book (or anywhere along the way) you decide that you need to call in the big guns for help (in your organization or personally), I'm here for you. Just email me at bridget@drbridgetcooper.com. Please don't be afraid to reach out for help because these phenomena are powerful and can send an organization into crisis in the blink of an eye. Like any cancerous condition, intervention is more effective at stage one than at stage four.

I've dedicated an entire chapter to each of the three "triple threats," but I'll define them briefly here so you know what to expect as you make your way through this book.

Stress: I think this is self-explanatory, but stress is the growing and ever-present phenomenon of feeling incapable of getting done what needs to get done or perform or feel the way you want to feel. Everyone everywhere can't seem to complain enough about how much stress they feel and how it negatively affects every aspect of their lives. I'm going to tackle the very definition of stress so that you can approach it from a novel stance and therefore eradicate its power over you.

Drama: Again, this is probably obvious to you if you've spent much time outside of your house (or even just breathing on the planet since the drama can come into your house via the internet). Drama is the exaggeration of normal human interactions that makes small problems bigger than they need to be by involving emotion, additional players, and widespread attention.

Isolation: This one is a bit less apparent, and, for the purposes of this book, it defined in two ways from two sources. Isolation has a physical and an interpersonal component. *Physical isolation* refers to the distance that people physically have from one another, whether that be because they are remote workers, in another location simply separated from their team, or on-site but with limited interaction with others. *Interpersonal isolation* can be affected by physical isolation ("I don't see you therefore we don't feel connected") but it can also be a stand-alone occurrence. Interpersonal isolation is the lack of belonging or connectedness you feel with your colleagues. The two sources of physical and interpersonal isolation can be self- or other-determined (or somewhere on that spectrum). For example, you may choose to be a remote worker or that may have been chosen for you. And, you may choose to be a loner or you may be intentionally shut out by your colleagues.

After we've thoroughly explored the problems and their origins, we're going to talk solutions. I'll offer all sorts of quick fixes and long-term strategies for ridding your life of unnecessary stress, drama, and isolation. I'll give you a short lesson on the five-step model for change, referring you to my book on the change process, **Stuck U.**, in case you'd like a separate guide. You'll find self-assessments throughout the book, as well as quotes that will drive home the lessons and practices I want you to incorporate into your daily life. Practice forms habit and habits form change.

"When another person makes you suffer, it is because he suffers deeply within himself, and his suffering is spilling over. He does not need punishment, he needs help.
That's the message he is sending." ~ Thich Nhat Hanh

All too often, potential clients approach me with misdiagnosed dilemmas they need me to tackle. Misdiagnosed? It's a natural, understandable mistake, really. It's something we do on a personal level day after day so why would work be any different? It's not different. We get mixed up between the symptom and the root problem. It's no wonder. In this crazy, fast-paced existence we live in, we are rewarded for efficiency. If something is happening and it's uncomfortable, we want to fix it fast or move on. We don't feel we have the time to tackle anything, especially not something as juicy and complicated as cultural circus antics.

Yeah, I'm not letting you go that easily! Nice try. It's not my first rodeo (or circus), people. I wrote a book about this, for crying out loud. Of *course* we are stopping to tackle this!

We spent some time discussing the problems that the triple threat of stress, drama, and isolation bring to organizations. We now need to document how these problems present themselves and where they come from. Because I'm all about fixing things, we will address the disorders that are creating the symptoms so we can solve them at the source. My mission for this book is to unearth some of the unhealthy patterns that have been ingrained in you being an inhabitant in our culture so you can make different decisions about what you think, feel, and do in response to them. If you're a corporate leader, this book will give you the ability to bring new messages, expectations, and practices to your organization so that it (and its employees) will be healthier as a result. (Of course, you'll call me if you need help making that happen....won't you?)

Key Chapter Concepts

- People have four core needs that demand to be filled or dysfunction ensues: Control, Connection, Purpose, & Validation

- The triple threat to corporate culture is comprised of Stress, Drama, and Isolation.

- It's helpful to note that the symptoms are not the cause.

"The secret of change is to focus all of your energy,
not on fighting the old, but on building the new." ~ Socrates

3

SWORD SWALLOWING

> "Knowing what's right doesn't mean much
> unless you do what's right." ~ Theodore Roosevelt

Every day in countless offices around the world, people are working harder just to maintain their current standard of living. They are living in constant fear of layoffs, downsizing, outsourcing, and mergers. The most pervasive feeling is one of powerlessness. Employees feel that they cannot change the situation because there is nothing that can be done, at least not anything in their control. Work becomes a circus, with no clear ringleader.

How are you benefitting from the so-called circus you're in at work? Wait, WHAT? That was a pretty audacious question, right? I'm brave, and insightful, like that. How many of us have stayed at a job, or in a relationship, regardless of how unhealthy or soul-sucking it was, just so we could remain safe and connected? So we could stay a part of something. A team or a tribe or a partnership. Or maybe we were getting something out of the negative situation, even though we were bitching uncontrollably about it. I've been studying and intervening on this dynamic for years and I'm crystal clear about this:

No matter what pain people profess to be in while struggling with a situation, they are always getting *something* out of it.

They are getting some need(s) met. They are receiving some reward. It might be self-defeating overall.

As we reviewed, the four core needs that are at play are **control, connection, purpose**, and **validation**, and they are required in varying intensities depending on the individual (i.e., "control freaks" or insecure people). Something in the dysfunctional pattern is meeting (some part of one or more of) their needs, so they persist with the behavior. The fact of the matter is that if they were literally getting nothing (healthy or unhealthy) out of it, they would walk away. There would be no reason to stay. I wrote a lot about getting needs met (either in a healthy or unhealthy way) in my first book, **Feed The Need**. People have a natural and compelling drive to get their needs met and will find ways (constructive or destructive) to do so. In an organization, if the culture is dysfunctional, people often resort to getting their needs met in destructive ways and the company (and everyone in it) pays the price.

What happens when things start to go sour but people remain? Well, if they are legitimately committed to fixing the situation, it's usually a good thing. All too often, unfortunately, people stay and become *part* of the problem. In order to function on any level in an organization, you're drawn into its dynamics. Have you ever tried yawning on a bus? Have you observed what happens? One person after another yawns, too. Yawning appears to be "contagious," but there isn't a "yawning virus" so what's the true explanation? It's based in the mirror-neuron system which basically creates a need to replicate something that we see in the environment.

The same thing sometimes goes for dysfunctional behavior: You see it and something is triggered in you to replicate it. Fitting into a group has evolutionary benefits: If you didn't fit in, you were left behind and you either starved to death or were eaten by a wooly mammoth. By copying (or simply accepting) bad behavior, you benefit by fitting in. The downside is that you're fitting into something that is broken. Plus, by fitting in, you join the ranks of the problem so, in fact, you make it worse. As I've told you, this book is your guide to figuring out how to think, feel, and act upon things differently so you can contribute to the solution instead of the problem.

"If you want your life to be different you have to start reacting to life differently." ~ Bryant McGill

Let's tackle an analysis of the problems first, shall we? I'm confident that I can convince you that solving them is worth the effort once you're able to see the cost to individuals and companies if they are left unaddressed.

Here are some of the ways that the workplace reveals itself as a chaotic, dysfunctional, toxic mess instead of a fluid, organized, thriving success:

- High turnover (high performers leave)
- Low turnover (poor performers stay)
- High absenteeism and work-related injuries
- Low-concentration (leading to high errors and/or accidents)
- HR faces ethics, harassment, bullying, and performance issues
- Low productivity
- Surging overtime
- Customer complaints
- Low morale

And in the worst of cases:

- Bullying culture
- Customer exodus
- Lawsuits
- Workplace violence
- Downsizing
- Bankruptcy

What do all of these have in common? They are diminishing and often destroying the potential that companies have for success and abundance. Since companies are made up of individuals, when companies fail, individuals suffer, too. Communities are affected, particularly when small or core businesses meet their demise. It is in our collective best interests to prevent as many failures as possible, especially businesses that are integral to local economies. Let's not overlook the fact that unhealthy workplaces are literally killing us, whether it be through violence on the job or stress-related illnesses.

Much like the circus, workplaces today have taken on an incredible life of their own. The parallels are striking. There are:

- The clowns who favor form over substance
- The drama-seeking tightrope walkers, fire eaters, and sword swallowers
- The chaotic monkeys who are all up in your business
- The lions who simultaneously need to be tamed and have their power harnessed
- The elephants that are smart and attractive but need to be guided
- The sideshow acts (do I really need to say more here?)
- The ringleader (or two or three or too many to count) who often isn't so great on the "leader" part of that.

The focus of this book is to reduce the experience and effects of stress, drama, and isolation.

Addressing those three things will foster an environment that reduces negative feelings, hostility, and aggravation. When you have a culture that supports open and honest communication, people are less stressed out and create less drama. When people are treated fairly and conflict is addressed calmly and not left to fester, the culture benefits. When employee's personal development (including understanding best practices for conflict resolution, effective communication, and stress management), work-life balance, and overall health are valued (not just in words on a catchy slogan on the walls of the company, but also backed up by deed), the culture is healthier. Together, these investments pay off in spades in lowering the toxicity of an environment because toxic workplaces support dangerous behavior.

"Difficulty is inevitable. Drama is a choice." ~ Anita Renfroe

~ The Pathways ~

Stress, drama, and isolation are connected and overlap with one another in a variety of ways. In order to be able to manage all of the topics, however, this book separates them into different chapters. Along the way, I'll point out some of those connections, but I'll start here with giving you a roadmap so you can draw some of these inferences on your own.

Stress leads to Drama	When you're stretched thin you are apt to react emotionally.
Stress leads to Isolation	Sometimes you shut people out when you're overloaded, choosing a task- vs. a people-focus.

Drama leads to Isolation	When someone is overly emotional they can get tossed from informal networks and be undermined by others.
Drama leads to Stress	Does this really need an explanation?
Isolation leads to Stress	Whether it's from bullying or another source, people need connections for social reasons and to get things done. When they can't, it gets stressful.
Isolation leads to Drama	When people are isolated, they are apt to act out to get their needs met.

Since all of these can be daisy-chained together, any one of these can lead to any other one. This is good for us to know so that we can anticipate issues, find root causes, as well as frame the best intervention to correct it.

Example

Ever have one of those weeks when you feel like the world is closing in on you? Like no matter where you turn, there's a new shit storm headed your way? I had one of those weeks and I was sure it was going to break me. Clearly it didn't since you're reading my book, but it came awfully close. Why? It struck me quite funny when I realized that the very themes that were kicking my butt personally were the themes that I was writing about in this book: Stress, drama, and isolation. Ready to hear how they played out and how I got out of my funk?

First off, everyone has stress in their life to a smaller or greater degree. We all have bills to pay, mouths to feed, bodies to care for, jobs to keep, and so on. Some of us have more on our plates. We have elderly parents, young children, chronic health issues, money struggles, mental health challenges, and toxic people in our personal and professional lives. When the stressors come knocking one right after the other, it can throw even the most relaxed and mentally strong person for a loop.

Now, let me share that I am a fixer. A helper. A rescuer. I make sure that my cape is always at the ready, even if I have no business trying to fly in the first place. Who cares? I got this! Where there's a will, there's a way! Boy, do I have will!!! I even have a few finely-honed ways to get to just about any solution. So, you can imagine that when I'm faced with a challenge that I can't fix, I can quickly turn into a hot, crazy mess. I've gotten better over the years, being much more selective in who I choose to put my cape on for, but I still sport it more often than I should.

At the time of my story, I had almost worn out my cape by being in rescue mode for over three years for a colleague of mine. He was my closest colleague by far, acting as a cheerleader, advisor, and confidante of mine for years. Being a sole proprietor can be lonely at times, but our relationship staved off those feelings because we carved an "office" for just us. Then he started to slip professionally. He lost assignments due to lack of focus and lackluster results. Whenever he had a crisis I was right there to coach or rescue him out of it. I'd referred him to jobs, helped him build a new entrepreneurial venture…the works. When he needed a loan, I was the Bank of Dr. Bridget. It was straining our relationship to the nth degree and I finally reached my breaking point and cut him off entirely. I still spoke with him, but it was from a distance.

He had been my key business advisor, so ousting him was really difficult from a practical and personal perspective. I was feeling pretty alone and removed from all of the comforts and support that a partnership like that provides (*isolation*). To make matters worse, I came to find out that he'd used my company credit card to charge personal expenses without my knowledge. If that wasn't enough, he'd confided some of his dishonesty to another one of my close colleagues (who then didn't tell me what was going on, effectively lying by omission) which created a stressful triangle between us (*stress*). Are you sensing the crazy that was taking over my brain? Wait! I'm not done! After I finished confronting my ousted colleague about his trespasses, I addressed my other close colleague. She got super defensive and (you may not believe this) posted her feelings about it on social media, tagging me in her comments(*drama*). Yeah, I know, I should have been writing a script for a soap opera.

I could feel myself sinking into sadness and quasi-paranoia. I knew I was being sensitive and controlling, but I couldn't help feeling like I'd gotten the raw end of a stacked deal. I had been lied to, evaded, and now blamed for overreacting. Amidst it all, I'd lost my closest confidante (effectively my unofficial business partner) and another close colleague in a matter of days. I wanted to see the growth opportunity in all of it (because that's what I DO), but I didn't have the bandwidth for it. I was in the midst of writing **this** book and I just couldn't take the time off to wallow in self-pity and pain. And, no, it was not lost on me that the book I was writing was on stress, drama, and isolation and I was neck-deep in all three. Funny, right? Not so much.

So what did I do? After I seriously considered checking myself into a "mental spa" for a few days to recalibrate and go through some sort of Zen overhaul, I turned to Facebook. This is often a really, really bad idea, to be honest, since it's *social media* and social media is a vortex in and of itself for stress, drama, and isolation. I could just write this entire book on how social media contributes to the circus!

But I digress.

I tried to stave off all of the nonsense that accompanies it by doing what I do best. I went into it with an intention: Not to stir up the drama, but to tackle the stress and isolation I was feeling. I posted a request for help. First and foremost, I made sure that the two involved parties couldn't read my post (I love privacy settings). I told everyone what I'm telling you, only scrubbed for social media (didn't share the story, just my current state of angst and lack of focus). I asked for help in getting motivated when I felt like my soul was being sucked dry. Talk about dramatic language, right? In a matter of hours, I had over 50 thoughtful, helpful, and even funny posts to get me out of my funk and back to the writing grind.

Unexpected (awesome) result: People who read the suggestions by others were also helped by them! I had strangers writing back and forth to each other in the comments section, offering guidance and support on their own struggles. It was amazing! Before the night was over, I was already back at the computer, typing furiously about the help I'd been given, knowing that it would benefit you when you find yourself mired in stress, drama, and isolation or any one of the three.

One of the posts suggested getting a witness to my writing; a person who could support me by being present with me while I pursued that creativity and channeling. I loved this! It was confirmation of the tenets of the work I do with clients around the world: That we crave connection with others. We need to be validated for the good work that we do and share with others. We are not islands, self-sustaining and self-serving. We gain energy from connecting with others, when those connections are healthy and solid. It is our work to eliminate toxic connections and build healthy ones.

"In times of great stress or adversity,
it's always best to keep busy, to plow your anger
and your energy into something positive." ~ Lee Iacocca

Here are just a few of the suggestions in case you find yourself procrastinating something because of stress:

- Just immerse yourself in the work now, edit or correct it later after the stress has passed.

- Talk out loud about it, write about it, meditate on it. Give the distraction, stress, etc. all of the roads out of your world. Use it as a spark to ignite your engine, harness its power for good.

- Take a run.

- Just nose down and do it. Look at the stressors later.

- Thank the stressors and move on. It'll still be there when you're done being awesome.

- Wallow in it…for a few, structured minutes. Then move on. Make bitch sessions literal bitch *sessions*.

- Have a good cry or scream session, preferably some place private where no one will become concerned and add "police report" to your laundry list of things to address later.

- Let it go. Just tell the stress that you're done with it and move on.

Good advice. I tried every one of those and they all worked to some degree. What did I learn in the process? From pain comes healing. Through struggle we find strength. And, by reaching out, we can best reach in.

Some other things I reflected on:

I realize that I had totally set myself up for most of it. They did what they did and they are clearly responsible for injuring me in the ways that they did. They lied by commission and omission. She minimized my experience and attacked me when she felt offended (and "caught"). He tried to be someone he wasn't by lying to me, and got close to my friend in a selfish, self-serving, duplicitous manner. All of those things are true. Yet, in the end, I brought myself into the situation and I am responsible for myself and no one else.

Let me throw those words at you again:

I am responsible for myself and no one else.

It's that pesky balance between being responsible for (**in control of**) yourself, yet still having other people contribute to (**influence**) your state of mind.

I brought the stress and drama and isolation to myself. That's the amazing and wonderful and best damn news in the world. You know why? Because that means:

I can send the stress and drama and isolation to a galaxy far, far away and out of my life any time I want!

Whatever you give power to, by giving it your focus, has the power. *Your* power. Don't allow that to happen.

You cannot control when a negative person or situation comes to you. You can control the amount of time you invest in it and how much energy you give to it. Say, "I see you" and "I give you no power over me." Offer it a tiny space to wither away and shrink from your world and your consciousness. Take all of the energy you now have left over to pour it into all the good that you can do, the things you can contribute to the world.

"If you don't like something, change it.
If you can't change it, change your attitude." ~ Maya Angelou

Now, the best idea is to not let this craziness come into my life in the first place. THAT would be a smarter plan. But, when it does enter my realm, I can pack its bags and send it on its merry way. As I like to say, "ain't nobody got time for that." And that nobody includes me.

Does it include you, too?

If so, read on and let's get this party started!

Key Chapter Concepts

- Stress, Drama, & Isolation are connected to and influence one another.

- They are costing companies millions of dollars in lost productivity, healthcare, and turnover.

- We are in control of our thoughts, feelings, and behaviors but others influence us.

"You will either step forward into growth or you will step back into safety." ~ Abraham Maslow

4

RINGS OF FIRE

"And now that you don't have to be perfect,
you can be good." ~ John Steinbeck

In thinking about work, complete the following sentence:

I'm so _____.

I'm hoping you wrote "awesome" or "lucky," but if you're like 99% of my clients, you probably wrote "busy" or "overworked" or "overwhelmed" or the summary word of all: STRESSED.

~ The Six-Letter "S" Word ~

The first element of the triple threat I'm tackling is stress. Stress is the number one complaint I hear from my clients, hands down. There aren't enough hours, resources, people, space, etc. to accomplish what's on the list. Companies are trying to do more with less and it's putting incredible pressure on people, and companies as a whole, to be more than they feel capable of being.

Stress is like a badge of honor. A perpetual condition we seem relegated to. In fact, if someone asks you about work (or life) and you don't include your level of stress they look at you sort of funny. Like, "how did you manage to THAT?" Or, better yet, "what are you ON?" More than ever before, the leading cause of stress for American adults is occupational. Since we know that stress is a major factor in illness and disease, we can safely say that work is legitimately killing us. The statistics are downright frightening. According to the National Institute of Safety and Health "Stress at Work" study:

- 40% of workers reported their job was very or extremely stressful.
- 25% view their jobs as the number one stressor in their lives.
- 75% of employees believe that there is more on-the-job stress than a generation ago.
- 29% of workers felt "quite a bit" or "extremely" stressed at work.
- 26% of workers said they were "often or very often burned out or stressed by their work."
- Job stress is more strongly associated with health complaints than financial or family problems.

Those who think that their workplace deals with employees unfairly are more prone to reporting poor health. That means, to some extent, that managers and executives can help to mitigate stress-related health issues, and that top-down efforts to foster a more collegial and secure working environment leads to happier and healthier workers. The research recommends company-wide events and mentorship programs to help in tackling high stress levels for employees and the associated health costs for employers. Efforts to retain employees for significant periods of time might help too, since workers tend to feel more secure and form more supportive social networks when there is some level of consistency within the employee pool, according to the research.

"Unprecedented financial pressures, and an ever-increasingly aggressive public culture, along with social, moral, and spiritual fragmentation, are leading to lives being overwhelmed by stress, intolerable interior isolation, and even quiet despair." ~ Sean Brady

Unfortunately, just because someone has the title of "boss" or some other leadership position doesn't mean that they are exempt from debilitating behavior. In some cases, it's more likely! So often I've witnessed people in power positions ignore their formal role when the going gets tough and becoming the equivalent of a 7-year old child who's had her favorite toy taken away from her.

Some of us forget to "act our parts," especially when stress sets in. As adults, we can do some pretty whacky, immature things when we find ourselves in stressful situation, even if they are of our own doing. Most commonly, we regress. We stomp our feet like toddlers, raise our voices, get sarcastic and biting, teary-eyed, selfish, and we might even find ourselves on the couch curled up in fetal position sucking our thumbs and clinging to our blankie. Unless our family members or friends are equipped to snap us out of our funk, this response isn't going to get us anywhere and no closer to alleviating the stress. In fact, taking on this helpless, self-defeating persona is most likely going to compound the problem.

According to the "Attitudes in the American Workplace" study:

- 80% of workers feel stress on the job.

- Close to 50% report they need help in learning how to manage their stress.

- 42% say their coworkers need help in learning how to manage their stress.

- 14% of respondents had felt like striking a coworker in the past year, but didn't.

- 25% have felt like screaming or shouting because of job stress.

- 10% are concerned about an individual at work they fear could become violent.

- 9% are aware of an assault or violent act in their workplace.

- 18% had experienced some sort of threat or verbal intimidation in the past year.

- The U.S. has the highest violent crime rate of any industrialized nation.

- An average of 20 employees are murdered each week, making homicide the second highest cause of workplace deaths and the leading cause for females.

- About 1,000,000 non-fatal violent crimes (sexual, others) occur at while on the job annually, which translates to 18,000 each week.

- The sad news is that the true figures are probably even more disturbing since it's assumed that many non-fatal violent crimes (especially sexual assaults) are not reported.

According to a 2015 working paper by Harvard and Stanford Business schools, health problems associated with job-related anxiety (hypertension, cardiovascular disease, mental health) account for more deaths each year (120,000) than Alzheimer's disease, diabetes, or influenza. That is stunning.

Anxiety about our jobs is literally killing us.

It's costing businesses a staggering amount of money, too. These stress-related health problems could account for $180 billion in annual healthcare expenses. That's a lot of money and a boatload of stress.

What is stress, anyway? Simply put,

Stress is the pressure felt when what you *want to control* is greater than *what you can actually control.*

Think about that for a minute. When you're feeling stressed because of an impending deadline at work, you're wanting to have more time than you have. You want to control the clock, but you can't. You want to create more hours between "now" and "then," but that's impossible. So, what do you do? You feel stress.

Consistent with this definition of stress, studies have shown that cardiovascular disease is linked to having little perceived control as compared to the number and level of demands placed upon people. When there is more on your "to do" list than there are hours in the day, you feel stress. Workload was rated the number one job-stress (46%) according to ComPsych's 2005 "StressPulse" survey. Workers stated that they were 20% more likely to make mistakes on the job as a result. When your success is dependent upon other people or factors, you feel stress. People issues accounted for 28% of job stress (ComPsych survey, 2005). When there are changes coming, you want to know how it's going to all play out, but you probably don't, so you feel stress. Because of the threat to job security, people who face downsizing get sick twice as frequently as those who feel more secure in their jobs.

> "Stress is nothing more than a socially acceptable
> form of mental illness." ~ Richard Carlson

In times of change at the workplace, "unclear expectations" are rated the top stressor (ComPsych survey, 2005). If you don't know what your boss expects of you, and your normal environmental cues are thrown off by the change that is happening, you are going to feel stress. More often than not, organizational leaders aren't practiced or confident in conflict and communication strategies.

When changes hit the scene, leaders are apt to get busy implementing and "handling" the change, forgetting that communication has risen to the top need of their employees. It's not just reports and memos and the dreaded "announcements." It's real, honest, forthright, detailed, interactive communication. People who are uncertain about the future crave it. They might not tell you directly, but they surely will indirectly. The dysfunction that arises from change centers around employees feeling out of the loop which translates into feeling disrespected, out of control, and untrusting. These all breed problems for organizations and require attention.

Stress isn't always a bad thing. Stress can push people to do their best, fast. Stress can invigorate people and shake them out of any haze they might have been in. Some people thrive under pressure, but usually in short bursts. It's like morning coffee: It serves you, just not all day long. The constant, elevated levels of stress are harmful to our physical and mental health because stress drives you to try to control something. According to Wikipedia:

> Stress hormones such as cortisol and epinephrine are released by the body in situations that are interpreted as being potentially dangerous. Cortisol is believed to affect the metabolic system and epinephrine is believed to play a role in ADHD as well as depression and hypertension. Stress hormones act by increasing heart rate, blood pressure, and breathing rate and shutting down metabolic processes such as digestion, reproduction, growth and immunity.

Consistent stress tires the body, mind, and spirit. People with the best of intentions, skills, and habits can definitely go off the rails when the pressure won't let up. It's like a tea kettle: It needs to release steam, or cut the heat, or it will literally explode. People are like tea kettles, my friend. We have breaking points and the scary thing is that you don't know what anyone's is in advance.

Entrepreneurs have to set their own limits because they are flying solo One such business owner I interviewed almost paid the ultimate price for not holding those limits.

> I was incredibly busy building my business, going quickly from a one-person shop to a small business. I was still doing all of the work, acting like a laborer. One day I found myself laying on a client's driveway with chest pains. I realized that I can't do it all. I can't be everything to everyone. I have to fill my tank first and keep a safe distance from some of the stressors. I have to trust that others will do their jobs, or face getting new people. My advice to other entrepreneurs is to work for the business then let the business work for you. Always be building your business with the intent to step away. Just like with kids, we need to teach our employees and the business itself how to live without us.

Speaking of exploding, "desk rage" and "phone rage" have also become increasingly common terms. For those of us familiar with playground brawls, these are the dressed up versions. When employees get stressed to their breaking points, they are known to explode, acting unprofessionally and creating a hostile work environment. It's even worse when the person has institutional power like the executive in my next example.

> I work in high-pressure, professional office in New York City. One of the managers in the office works crazy hours and has been nicknamed "Mount Vesuvius" because of her temper. When someone has to deliver bad news to her at the end of the quarter, her subordinates have been known to "draw straws" to decide who has to do it. Why? She's a beast at crunch time and she's been known to scream at us when we tell her something she doesn't like. Her emails are caustic and she's hung up on me several times. Her behavior is tolerated because she's got that magical mix of skills, knowledge, and contacts in the industry. She makes coming

to work so stressful. If I could find another job with similar benefits, I would in a heartbeat.

How sad is that? I wish I could say that this story is uncommon, but it's not. It's happening everywhere. When the person is in a supervisory position and treating their subordinates like this, I call it "management by abuse." It stresses everyone in their midst and provides a hotbed of litigation potential, not to mention opening the door to workplace violence.

"Humans are much weaker than you think. Because they are weak, sometimes they become cruel." ~ Master Gong Dal

In the following example, the company took a strong stand which most likely saved it from a lawsuit at a minimum and a violent outburst at maximum.

I had a co-worker who was obsessed with his ex-wife. He raged about her constantly at work, slamming his fists on his desk whenever he corresponded with her via email. The most disturbing thing about his behavior is that he would go from yelling at one of us (or about her), red in the face, fists and jaw clenched one minute and then pick up the phone and talk to a customer happy as can be, like he was skipping through daisies. The flip of that switch was alarming. I told my manager about it, but it wasn't until a group of us made our concerns known that they finally fired the guy. I don't know what ever happened with his ex-wife, but I find myself praying for her.

This is serious stuff, my friends. Serious. Had this company not terminated him and he had taken out his rage at work, the company clearly would have been liable. Too often, companies are worried more about the legal action they might face from the terminated employee and less about the legal (and safety) repercussions from their co-workers. Not only does this create a hostile work environment but it empowers those who behave badly. If there are no consequences for acting like that, why would they audit their own behavior? To be fair, they might not audit their behavior either way, but as members of an organization (and society), we have to intervene. We are compelled to set a standard of behavior. We have to stand up to the culture of incivility that we have slipped into. I really have to believe that we are better than that. I also fully contend that we have the resources and insight to pave a different path forward. The framework and tips are in this book so please pay attention and bring them into the world.

Stepping off of my soapbox now. For *now*. It's time to tackle violence before it tackles you.

~ Violence ~

Workplace violence is a complicated phenomenon. In order to keep it clear, I need to take some time to speak about violence *outside* the workplace that all too often leads to violence *at* the workplace. I'm talking about domestic violence. Why should you as an executive be concerned with domestic violence? It's "domestic" not "workplace" so why do you need to worry about it at all? Easy. Domestic violence spills over into the workplace in a host of ways, costing companies productivity, effectiveness, and cold, hard cash. Domestic violence accounted for over one fourth (27%) of violence in the workplace. According to the U.S. Department of Labor, victims of domestic violence (and, yes, this includes men) are likely to have:

- Attendance problems
- Decreased productivity
- Inconsistent work patterns

- Concentration challenges
- Safety issues
- Poor health and hygiene
- Unusual/changed/disruptive behavior
- Depression
- Drawing on supervisor's time

If you suspect that one of your employees may be a victim of domestic violence, for their welfare and that of your company's, you are strongly advised to inquire and offer support and counseling referrals.

The best defense is a good offense so working to prevent workplace violence is a better strategy than reacting to it when it happens. Some workplace violence is random and can't be foreseen, but there are myriad stories of situations where there were plenty of warnings as well as a pathway of problems that could have predicted it. There are definitely things we can do to reduce the risk, and at the same time, benefit the health of our corporate culture.

As a former human resources professional, I have a special appreciation for interpersonal issues, but I was shocked when I researched the statistics on some of these phenomena.

Did you know?

- Workplace violence is responsible for two MILLION non-fatal injuries each year.
- Homicides at the workplace are the leading cause of death at work, with over 1,000 homicides each year, according to statistics collected by the U. S. Department of Justice.
- 35% of workers reported being bullied in the workplace with 62% of the bullies being men. The clear majority of bullies were supervisors and executives. 40% of those being bullied

never reported it to their employer. Of those that reported the bullying, 62% reported that they were ignored. Targets of bullying are, somewhat surprisingly, competent, accomplished, and experienced employees, translating into a "kill or be killed" attitude on the part of the bully. Some estimates of the financial costs of bullying are over $200 billion per year in job-related stress, absenteeism, and attrition (Workplace Bullying Institute).

Some of this violence is from the public or from employees' personal connections (spouses, stalkers, family members), but bullying is clearly a phenomenon at work. Further, there is certainly a portion of the violent acts that are committed by employees against other employees and bullying can give rise to that violence.

Bullying is defined as a "conscious repeated effort to wound and seriously harm another person not with violence, but with words and actions" (Williams, Psychology Today, 2/21/15). The intent is to destroy the target's self-confidence which is just a tactic that serves to reduce the target's power and influence so that the bully can garner more of it.

Just like the bullies we met on the playground, bullies want to tear you down so that they can conversely build themselves up. Sometimes the bullying is subtle and hard to pinpoint like excluding you from meetings and conversations, taking credit for your work, and openly criticizing and/or humiliating you in front of others. Sometimes it's more direct like when they browbeat, threaten, insult, and yell at you. Words that apply to bullying behavior include: systematic, hostile, threatening, abusive, humiliating, intimidating, and sabotage. Bottom line: Bullies are intentionally trying to harm you by interfering with your ability to do your work effectively.

"Bullies are just men who don't know
they are cowards, of course." ~ Antonia Hodgson

Bullying can be a form of poorly handled stress, displaced control, inherent jealousy and insecurity. For some, it is a character flaw, reinforced by an environment that has at best tolerated it and at worst encouraged it. For others, it is a poor adaptation to stress.

I know, I know, you want me to explain that bold statement!

Going back to our discussion on stress: Stress is all about control. Stress is caused by the difference between that which we want to (believe we can) and that which we can actually control. Stress, in low and brief doses, can be instrumental in getting us off the dime and set into motion. Excess or constant stress does a number on a host of things: our immune system, nervous system, cardiovascular system, and mental health. When we are stressed, we often regress to old, familiar patterns of behavior which usually aren't an example of our *best* behavior.

It can be a challenge to be on our best behavior, to be thoughtful and considerate when our nerves are fried, we are over tired, and there's more to do than there are hours in a day. It's a perfectly human response to be cranky and short-tempered under the circumstances. Please don't get me wrong: I'm not excusing bad behavior, I'm simply acknowledging where it comes from. If we don't understand it we have little hope for fixing it. Sometimes "cranky" and "short-tempered" is not a big deal, made less of an issue by an apology and if you have solid relationships with the people you may snap at or in front of. Everyone has a bad day every now and then. If you make a habit of responding this way under stress, you're likely to tax your relationships and create quite a reputation for yourself.

Plus, you might even get accused of being a bully.

What exactly does it mean to be a bully?

I can speak for myself and say that when the term started being bandied around a few years back, the first image that came to my mind was of a little boy on the playground who threw sand at me and called me mean names, or knocked scrawny Billy down because he could. In the past, bullying usually referred a form of physical intimidation: You were afraid of a bully because the bully could physically injure you.

Today, bullying encompasses so much more than tussle on the playground. According to the Workplace Bullying Institute (2014):

> Workplace bullying is repeated, health-harming mistreatment of one or more persons (the "targets") by one or more perpetrators (the "bullies"). It's abusive conduct that is: threatening, humiliating, or intimidating; work interference (e.g., sabotage) which prevents work from getting done; and verbal abuse. [www.workplacebullying.org]

Bullying isn't the bad mood that comes and goes, although there is intermittent behavior that can be bullying in nature. It doesn't usually rise to the level of the textbook definition of bullying as described above though. At the core of this repeated behavior is a desire to control another person. As was discussed earlier in this chapter, taking control is a way to reduce your fear and anxiety. - Bullying alleviates this fear and anxiety by putting the bully in charge of more components of their environment.

"No one heals himself
by wounding another." ~ Ambrose of Milan

If bullying was a rare and inconsequential occurrence, it wouldn't have become a staple in our current workplace narrative. Yet, it has, and for good reason.

VitalSmarts conducts leadership research and recently published their findings on bullying (emotional and physical), which included 2,000 corporate employees:

96% stated that they had witnessed bullying at work.

27% reported that they work with someone who "browbeats, threatens, or intimidates others."

4% stated that they work with someone who "physically intimidates or assaults others."

One in five respondents stated that "coping with a bully costs them seven or more hours per week in extra work."

Because executives are concerned about the bottom line, let's tackle the financial one. How is that "extra work" statistic possible? What would this extra work consist of? Since bullying behavior can be overt or covert, targets can be openly bullied or it can be more subtle as in the withholding of resources (information, relationships, budgets, manpower). Bullying costs the targets (and any caught in the crossfire) time, energy, and resources (including money) due to, at the very least, inefficiency. If you have to trouble yourself to find a way around a bully, overcome the emotional burden of the bullying, and/or navigate the factions that are often created by people siding with the bully or the target, you're wasting precious time, focus, and resources.

To assign a number to it, if bully is costing seven hours per week for 20% of the workforce, and we assume an average wage of $40,000 per year, that's the equivalent of $8,000 per worker per year. If you have 500 employees, that's $800,000 per year of lost wages spent on being bullied. Pure insanity. Bottom line: Bullying is costing business a staggering amount of cold, hard cash, not to mention job satisfaction. From one affected professional:

I had to leave my last job because it was causing so much emotional stress that my mental and physical health were being negatively impacted. I felt stuck for a few years, as no other opportunities arose that made sense (lower pay, bigger commute, lose rank in seniority of the union, etc.). Then, an in-district opportunity arose, and I took it. Many former colleagues are wanting out, but feel stuck for the same reasons. Other, newer employees with less at risk, have left. I tried to address the issues with the bully head on and through mediation, but there was no long-lasting result. She makes many people feel the same way, and her personality will not change. Nobody understands why management keeps her and gives her positive reviews, despite being aware of her behavior and lack of professionalism. It feels like bad behavior is overlooked or rewarded, while good workers and teachers are taken for granted. Many of the good people are leaving because of poor management, which has led to extremely low morale. Everyone is hoping the administrators will retire or leave soon.

"People who repeatedly attack your confidence and self-esteem are quite aware of your potential,
even if you are not." ~ Wayne Gerard Trotman

~ Change & Bullying ~

How are change and bullying connected? What does change have to do with bullying?

Over the years, we have seen an exponential increase in reports of bullying behavior. Bullying in the workplace has become such a common occurrence that it's part of our national dialogue. Simultaneously, change has become part of our global experience.

We are in a constant state of flux. Change is a daily phenomenon, some of it anticipated and some of it comes out of left field. The one thing we can count on aside from death and taxes is change.

There are very few people out there who can truthfully say that they love change. I've found when I've interviewed people about their comfort level with change and when I press more, I find that they enjoy (or simply tolerate) change when they are in control of it. When people feel like they are in charge of the scope and timing of the change, it becomes a lot less daunting. Even then, we tend to approach change like a rabid animal: With extreme caution.

What can this book do for you, aside from sharing this ugly truth? It will guide you on how to:

- Avoid being a bully by addressing your need for control in other ways.
- Help others identify what bullying is and what it isn't so it's not a taboo term.
- Recognize the toll that bullying takes on the target's self-confidence and help them to rebuild it.
- Identify, intervene upon, and report it.

> "People don't stop being bullies when they grow up.
> They just dress differently to fool you." ~ Patti Digh

In its worst form, bullying satisfies the bully's urge to dehumanize the target, thereby justifying the harsh treatment. When a target is seen as inhuman it's no small wonder that the potential for danger rises. Even if it doesn't become physical, the emotional toll is great. For those executives out there thinking that once the bully is gone, the problem is over, think again. In domestic violence research it's been concluded that emotional abuse leaves more lasting, damaging scars than physical abuse. Since bullying at work is tantamount to emotional abuse, the effects on employees – and the culture – are significant and perpetual. When people are recovering from emotional trauma they are likely to have physical ailments, thereby increasing healthcare costs, absenteeism, and lower productivity.

What should you do if you think you're being bullied? Before you get confrontational or accusatory, I recommend you take a step back and follow a process that has a chance of changing things for you.

First, set an intention. Do you want to resolve this? Would you only be satisfied if the person didn't work with you? Are you open to options or are you fixated on only one resolution? Get clear on your agenda (if you have one) before you start or you're apt to get frustrated and add to the stress, drama, and potential isolation.

Second, really look at the situation. Assess what's going on. Consider if you've done all that you can do to resolve it. For example, have you pointed out the person's behavior *to the person*? Most people I speak with have spoken to *everyone but* the alleged bully. I'm not saying that bringing their behavior to their attention is fool proof, but it's a necessary first step.

Third, make sure you're keeping accurate records of the bullying behavior. Don't embellish the details. Speak the facts and note if there were any witnesses to the behavior. Again, we want to keep it as calm and clear as possible because calm equals power. Right or wrong, getting emotional diminishes your power.

Fourth, don't take this behavior laying down. Sometimes all it takes for a bully to back off is to stand up for yourself. They may wake up to their behavior or they may simply find another target. If targets keep standing up for themselves, the bully will eventually run out of targets and either behave better or leave.

Fifth, make sure you bring your supervisor (and human resources) up to speed on your experience. Resist being dramatic, but be clear. You'll be more credible the calmer and more fact-based you are.

If all else fails, let your feet do the walking. You deserve to feel safe, engaged, and valued and that may require that you find another company where you can contribute your time, energy, and talents.

The occurrence of bullying can be tied directly back to the Fear-Trust-Control model. How? Let's discuss, shall we?

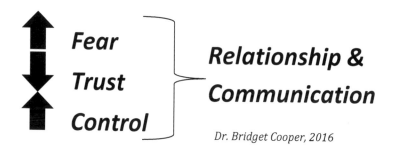

Dr. Bridget Cooper, 2016

This diagram is pretty intuitive. Well, at least the left side with the pretty arrows spelling it out for you.

When fear is high, trust is low.

When trust is low, fear is high.

When fear is high and trust is low, people try to exert control over anything and everything they can in order to feel more secure in the environment.

Make sense? If you don't trust your manager, you'll be fearful about every interaction, communication, and assignment, just waiting for the other shoe to drop. In response, you'll try to control everything down to the minutest detail. This is our natural response to fear: control. Some clients have told me that they aren't "afraid" so this model doesn't fit for them. Being the student of human behavior that I am, I accept this as truth, for them. They may not be aware of fear for a whole host of reasons. Perhaps fear isn't an emotion that they feel comfortable owning for themselves. Sometimes when I change the word "fear" slightly to a more palatable word like, "uncertainty" they accept it.

If you're interacting with someone who says they aren't afraid, look to see if they appear anxious or excitable: That's a telltale sign that they are feeling fearful. The other way that fear often reveals itself is in anger or hostility. I've found that fear is seen by some as a form of weakness whereas anger or hostility is seen as powerful so people, usually subconsciously, choose to display the fear that way.

Now the address the right side of the model:

When fear is high, trust is low, and control efforts are exaggerated to deal with the fear and distrust, the only saving grace is relationship and communication. We can only navigate our way out of this quagmire the way we got into it: through relationship (focusing on building it versus negating or disregarding it) and communication (by creating healthy, open, positive communication instead of what we've probably *been* doing).

"The enemy is fear. We think it is hate,
but it is fear." ~ Gandhi

~Training the Sideshow Acts ~

Reducing stress can be accomplished in a variety of ways.

Be in the moment. One of the most common triggers that catapults people into stress, drama, and isolation is founded on a very Buddhist principle: Being in a moment other than the present one. Our tempo in this day and age is fast and furious, leaving little time for reflection and planning. We are rewarded for racing to the next meeting, appointment, or event without pause. The busier we are, the more important we feel and seem.

Take a breath. There are very few times in life when something requires your immediate and comprehensive attention. Yet, all too often, we receive an email or a text and feel compelled to jump on it. It's like it demands a response right there and then. Guess what, people? It doesn't. If you're clear-headed and the drama-meter is a two, by all means, respond. If not, press the pause button when you start to feel upset, taking a few deep breaths to get centered. You can feed the drama and stress or you can starve it. If you engage with others when you're not completely calm and focused, you're offering up a picnic lunch to it. My advice: Put that craziness on a starvation diet.

Reach out for <u>positive</u> help. When you're starting to stress, invite drama, or retract into isolation, it's time to reach out and get assistance from your circle of friends, family, and colleagues. Selecting **who** to reach out to and **how** is critical. All too often, we reach out to those who will blindly back us up and tell us how terrible our situation is and how someone else is to blame for our pain. It's like a little gang where the members are picking their target and getting ready to pounce. The only issue with that is that the group is likely to miss your contribution to the problem. Without seeing what you did to bring the situation to life, you:

- miss an incredible growth opportunity.
- will likely contribute to perpetuating the problem because your influence in it will be alive and well.
- may make it worse by involving more people on your "side" which will polarize the "sides."

"If you're letting your enemies bring you into
their unnecessary drama you're giving them
too much power over you and your emotions." ~Sonya Parker

Set clear expectations that are consistent with reality. First off, let me be clear: I love dogs. I use them as fodder for a lot of my narratives but it's only because they are so easy to relate to and we often are a lot like them in our motivations. One day not too long ago, one of my dogs managed to get up on our dining room table, knock what was left of my daughter's ice cream cake off of the table and consume a large portion of it, blue frosting and all. About 24 hours later, my dog's bowels mimicked Mount Vesuvius. I kid you not. She literally exploded. All over my house. It was the middle of winter and most of my windows were wide open as we tried to exorcise this demonic-like invasion of our beloved pooch. This went on for about twelve hours. She was miserable. We were all miserable, let me assure you.

One might think that this fifth-layer-of-Hell experience would deter my dog from getting into food that wasn't hers to eat in the future. Nope. Not a chance. One DAY later she climbed up onto that same table and attempted to stick her canine snout into a NEW birthday cake I'd just made to celebrate my daughter's birthday on her actual birthday.

The cake I made was epic. It was one of those Pinterest-inspired cakes that didn't even look real but it looked so damned yummy that my daughter begged me to make it.

When I heard the scratching noises coming from the dining room where the cake was atop our table, I ran from two rooms away like there was a burgeoning fire. It felt like I was in slow motion as I yelled, "nooooooooo" while sprinting to scare the dog off the table before she sank her muzzle into my beautiful masterpiece.

Luckily, my mommy ninja hearing and pursuit skills saved the day, but it gave me pause. I realized that I violated the very tenet that I preach the world over:

Never trust a dog to watch your sandwich.

Just a day after my beloved canine consumed my daughter's ice cream cake after climbing up on that SAME TABLE, I let her roam around the house with THIS new cake in that EXACT SPOT.

Was it the dog's fault that we almost lost another cake to her voracious curiosity and appetite. Nope. Not a chance. The responsibility was all mine. I know this dog, her patterns, her belligerence when it comes to getting something she wants. Instead of taking precautions to make sure that when she acted on her impulses she could cause no harm, I left her to her own devices. And what is a dog going to do when left to their own devices? Exactly what she did! They are going to get into trouble, eat the wrong things, scatter your belongings, run around the neighborhood, and probably pee on your rug.

People are just like dogs. Just. Like. Dogs. We do what we are inclined to do. We can only be trusted to be ourselves. To act out of need when our needs are deep. To behave in ways that seek to meet those needs.

If you don't want the mess, don't invite it in. Most of us can see a train wreck coming from a mile away, yet there are those of us who think we have super powers and can stop it like Superman, mid-crash. Yeah, no. We can't. It doesn't stop us from trying, but if we were smart it would. You're not in for a smooth journey if you spend your time trying to fix other people's lives. You've got your hands full just keeping a lid on your own neuroses, frustrations, and idiosyncrasies. Let other people manage theirs while you focus on your own.

I'm not proposing that you refuse to help others who request your help because we don't get through this life without a little help from others at times. I know from experience that "helping" can go awry, quickly and quietly. One day you're "helping" someone with a challenge and the next day you've become seemingly responsible for their mental, emotional, and financial health. It's a slippery slope, folks, so resist the impulse whenever you can to save another human being unless it's from immediate physical danger. Offer them the tools and advice so that they can help themselves, but you're not doing them any favors by taking care of their shit for them.

~ Summary ~

Stress is literally killing us, and workplace stress is at the center of our undoing. As leaders, we are compelled to assess, discuss, and communicate its damaging effects, including bullying and violence. We are called upon to resist accepting it as the norm. We have the tools to intervene upon it by addressing the root causes and not simply the symptoms. It's time to close down the circus, folks. High time.

Before we move on, take a moment to journal as to what you can do to reduce the stress in your life. Who can you pay less attention to? Where can you fit in moments to pause? What positive things can you increase in your routine that will give you strength?

Key Chapter Concepts
- Stress at work is literally killing us.
- Stress is the difference between what you seek to control and that which you can control
- 96% of employees have witnessed bullying at work and it costs U.S. businesses millions if not billions each year in lost productivity, turnover, etc.
- Change increases stress
- Understanding the Fear-Trust-Control model is essential to understanding stress.

"Life is not a matter of having good cards but of playing a poor hand well." ~ *Robert Louis Stevenson*

5

MONKEY BUSINESS

"If you know your enemy and yourself then
every battle is won." ~ Park Tae Seo

When I first conceived of this book, people stopped dead in their tracks at the mention of the word "drama." It was like I'd hit a nerve that every person on the planet could relate to. Drama at work is a ridiculously common occurrence and its destructive effects can paralyze businesses.

How drama shows up:

- Gossip/rumor mill, passive-aggressive patterns

- Emotional responses to emails, outbursts in meetings

- Stalemates, roadblocks, camps formed

- Human resource complaints

Unfortunately, we all know about gossip and the rumor mill. If you're in a workplace, chances are that there is an informal network of relationships that governs the information pipeline. To make a point, I'm going to pick on a certain job but please know that I have the utmost respect for the people who take on the daunting task of managing corporate executives. In a classic, traditional structure, the administrative assistants to the C-level executives are the ones most in the know. They see things coming and going, and are usually in those positions because of their level of discretion.

Except when they're not. Confidentiality is often thrown to the wolves if one of these admins has a personal relationship with people in other parts of the organization. They might tip their proverbial hat in order to protect a friend who benefits from being informed.

When I interview executives about their circus at work, they are quick to tell me all about the drama that engulfs their office environment. They share stories and anecdotes that make their business sound more like the halls of the local high school than a professional office. The interpersonal dynamics are full of dysfunction and disorder which is sucking the life out of the productivity, efficiency, and effectiveness that they could realize and benefit from.

I ask them a simple, yet profound question (because that's just my nature):

Are you *feeding* or *starving* the drama?

If you're handing over your power by reacting from emotion instead of responding from intention, you're feeding it. If you're putting ego needs in front of company demands, you're feeding it. If you're making the mission of the organization and the health of the people in it your first priority, you're starving it. If you're taking time to process your response to anything that comes your way, you're starving it.

Let's suppose that one of your colleagues comes to your office to complain about a fellow co-worker. Feeding the drama might include adding your own complaints to their list and creating inside jokes about and a nickname for your co-worker. Starving the drama would mean that you'd ask your colleague if they had talked with the fellow co-worker, and perhaps suggesting interventions to resolve the issue.

What if you don't feed the drama as I described above, yet you don't starve it the way I suggested either. I'll be blunt: If you're not starving it, then you're not part of the solution; so, you're part of the problem. Choose wisely.

"Above all, be the heroine in your own life,
not the victim." ~ Nora Ephron

One common drama builder comes from violating the following rule:

Praise in public, criticize in private.

When you're called out in front of others it's very frustrating. Our natural instinct is to protect our egos and go on the offense or the defense. We're inclined to attack (criticize) the person delivering the criticism or defend ourselves, often by taking on the victim stance. This dance is incredibly undermining to getting good business done. What could have started off as the identification of a problem has gotten transformed into an emotionally-charged interaction. When this happens, people quickly lose sight of the actual problem to solve and start positioning against one another, creating lines and alliances and all sorts of destructive cultural nonsense.

Example:

> Prior to a major layoff (8 of 11 in my department were fired, leaving myself and 2 others), our team was highly dysfunctional. Everyone blamed everyone else for problems and errors. Nobody wanted to help each other. The second in command tried to get us to rat each other out all the time. I had to disengage to stay sane. I would sit at my desk and put my earphones in so that I wouldn't hear my coworkers (literally) yelling at each other and being rude to each other in the middle of our row of cubes. It was humiliating. Most of the time I didn't even have music on; I was just trying to look like I wasn't involved in what was going on so nobody would ask me whose side I was on. I job shopped and got another offer at another company, however the layoff happened and I was 1 of the 3 that still had a job. I ended up staying because (1) I got a pay raise that was almost equal to what the new job offer was and (2) I really liked the new hires.

"The ability to summon positive emotions during periods of intense stress lies at the heart of effective leadership." ~ Jim Loehr

When the going gets tough and drama gets cranking, it can be hard not to jump into the deep, shark-infested waters with the drama royalty (notice how I didn't say "queens" since I've seen plenty of this behavior from men and women alike). I said it's "hard" but not "impossible." What can make it easier? A surefire, tested tactic I like to call, "Stop, Center, Move."

~ Dr. B. Says "Stop!" ~

First, take a deep breath. You're not going to solve anything being tense and running around like a chicken with your head cut off. I know, I know, that's the norm these days, but since when was it fun to be "normal?" I have a much better option for you. Go against the tide and get calm when the rest of the world is going crazy. When you're called to engage in drama, don't. How? Enact "Stop, Center, Move."

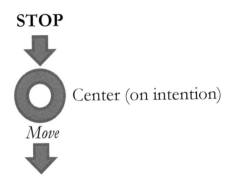

STOP

Center (on intention)

Move

What does this mean? It's like the old, "stop, drop, and roll" only this time the fire is in your head. The approach is directed at your behavior by way of your thoughts and feelings. It's a simple, three-step process to employ when you're transitioning between any activities, especially if there is an activity or situation that may trigger off stress or drama. **Stop** doing whatever you're doing, reading whatever you're reading, thinking whatever you're thinking. Just **stop**. Be still. If you're in public and you feel like it'll look weird for you to get all meditative in the midst of things, do something mindless like playing with your pen or getting a drink at the water fountain (I call it the "bubblah" but I didn't want to confuse those of you not raised in New England).

Once you've stopped (turn your phone over, for goodness sake!), then you can **Center**. **Center** is about setting an intention for the next moment or interaction you face. What do you want to bring to the next situation, meeting, conversation, etc.? Do you want to bring calm? Clarity? Insight? Challenge? Resolution? Pause on that thought, take a deep breath (or two) and focus on the feeling that the intention gives to you. In the centering, if you have time, challenge the thought that got you to your frustration.

Once you've gotten calm and focused on your intention, then and only then can you **Move**. It takes the novice maybe a minute to do this, the pros have it down in 15 seconds or less. Please don't tell me that you don't have time. You're in a rush. You've got places to be. You're already late for your next meeting. Your phone is buzzing. Someone must talk with you right now.

Respectfully, knock it off. Seriously. Unless someone is about to start WWIII and you're the only one who can intervene, you have a minute to Stop, Center, Move. I take that back. If you're the one who's been tasked to save the world, you'd BETTER Stop, Center, Move. We need you calm, focused, intentional, and attentive.

Stop, Center, Move offers:

1) **Awareness**: Observing our own thoughts, particularly as those thoughts precede the feeling-behavior sequence, and
2) **Power of the Pause:** The space between the thought-feeling-behavior sequence.

In setting your intention, make sure you're intending something that benefits the greater good, the organization, and/or the customer. Then, ask yourself:

"What does this situation require of me?"

Not, what do you want to do (which may involve throwing a coffee mug at your colleague)....what is required of you in order for your intention to be reached? What's the underlying issue that is being highlighted by the criticism and/or the overall situation? Your response needs to come from your head, your intellect, not your guts.

Example

I used to be very motivated to do work, not even because the work was meaningful but just because I am proud of myself when I do my best job. Now, due to drama between "teammates" and a lack of leadership, I am completely disenchanted with the entire non-profit field.

By responding with emotion, you're seeking to have your needs met (which is valid), but in the wrong context. It's not going to happen. You're setting yourself – and everyone else – up for failure and disappointment. It's a fool's errand and it hands your power over to others, presumably others that have no business being trusted with your feelings or experience. It's one thing to be vulnerable and put yourself out there, taking a risk to see if your needs get met. It's another matter entirely to do that when the problem is that the people you're presenting your needs to are incapable or unwilling to help you.

"Sometimes the most important thing in a whole day
is the rest we take between two deep breaths." ~ Etty Killesum

~ Fear Connection ~

Drama at work emanates from fear. All of the downsizing and reorganizations that have occurred left a scar of sorts on the minds of employees. So many of us relate to our jobs with fear and a sense of declining resources. There's never enough time, money, or personnel to do the things that are expected of us. It's rare to hear of anyone (aside from hourly employees) working fewer than 50 hours per week. It's commonplace in Corporate America to work 60-70 or more hours per week. Our cell phones are constantly attached to us; we are never more than a few minutes away from the next professional demand. We are literally glued to our work, 24/7. We sleep with our phones next to our heads.

We are mesmerized by this constant access, believing that if we don't respond right away that things will fall apart. Our own importance is elevated to unparalleled levels. We are convinced that the world will somehow stop if we don't finish the latest project or follow up on that recent email. That, in and of itself, is dramatic. It feels true because of demands placed on us. We are at a breaking point.

"An army of deer led by a lion is more to be feared
than an army of lions led by a deer." ~ Phillip of Macedonia

Speaking of contributing to that breaking point: Please don't even get me started on Facebook. A client recently shared the following drama that kicked up a notch (or twelve) on this social media mogul.

We have a team at work that isn't behaving at all like a team. It's every person for themselves. When assignments come to the department and one person (usually me) is getting the lion's share of the work, all you can hear are crickets when help is requested to share the load. Our boss calls us into discuss the issues we are having and guess what? More crickets. My "team" members chatter on and on before the meeting that they are going to tell him what's what and confront our boss with all of their complaints, but are silent in the meeting. Their passive aggressive behavior knows no limits! A few hours after our meeting where we discussed sharing the load and distributing the work more evenly among us, one of my "team" members posted a meme on Facebook about lazy co-workers who don't do their fair share but expect other people to do their work for them. The nerve! I posted a meme of my own about what teamwork actually means. It just never ends!

Unfortunately, this happens every day on a small and large scale. Even if your office mates aren't connected on Facebook, the passive aggressive antics are abundant across email, in meetings, and at the water cooler. Opposing camps are formed, lines are drawn, eyes are rolled, and projects are undermined. The cost to business is nearly impossible to calculate and depressing to contemplate. People are so busy carrying on in this high school-like soap opera that the work often takes a backseat. If you're yelling at the book right now saying, "it's not like that in my company! I work HARD and get to my work!" allow me to ask you one question: Would you get more and higher quality work done if people actually worked TOGETHER toward a common goal? You bet your ass you would!

~ Resistance Failure ~

What you resist persists.

I'm a can-do girl. I can tackle anything. Put a challenge in front of me and watch me rise to meet and exceed it. When personal issues confront and trigger me, I go into solution mode. No one can give me a problem I can't find my way out of. My parents relied on me so I'd BETTER be able to figure stuff out. I'm so good at resisting. When I can't immediately overcome something, I struggle like a fish out of water trying to form it to my will. "There just HAS to be a way!" I think I watched too many hero movies growing up and have difficulty accepting that some things just need to be witnessed, not conquered.

That's a hard truth to swallow for a fixer and a solution-focused healer like myself. It's like having a cure for cancer but not having a way to dispense it, so you watch as the cancer spreads and consumes its victim. Hell, no! Ain't nobody got time for THAT! Bridget's here to save the day! Alas, sometimes you just can't fix it. Sometimes it's not yours to fix. So many, many times it's not yours to fix. Bearing witness allows you to decide if it's yours or not and if it's worth it to try to fix or not. I'm not advocating taking a backseat in your own life: I'm advocating sitting on the side of the road and taking in the sights sometimes before you decide if you'd like to drive or ride along, and where you're headed in the first place.

Ever find yourself somewhere, emotionally or physically, and have no clue how you got there? Practicing awareness versus blind ambition allows you to be conscious of the path you're choosing.

Example

Things can go tragically wrong when relationships fail in a family business. This next story depicts what happens when a marriage sours and a business is trapped in their midst. Employees are forced to choose sides, one partner exits out and is blamed for all of the prior failures. Fingers are pointed, lines are drawn, aspersions are cast, and the clients suffer. Some spouses walk away to "avoid conflict and stress" and just end up with more of it down the line. Resentments set in, camps formed, etc.

When friends are business partners, it's much like marriages gone south, but can sneak up more quickly on you. Additionally, there aren't divorce property laws to protect or represent you or to help you to negotiate your way to a fair outcome when it's with a friend. So what does that mean for engaging in business with friends? Formalize everything. Document everything. It's business first, friendship second…really in order to put the friendship first. People resist formalizing things upfront but then end up with one partner taking advantage of the other, intentionally or unintentionally, citing things like disproportionate effort or investment, employee or client preference (one manager over the other), or blaming each other for failures or holding back from a different vision. When you start there is liberal trust. Over time, the business may stress you or your partner and distrust starts to take hold, especially if fear starts to rise (economic challenges, etc.). This leads to an imbalance in control (one taking more or both vying for top-dog status) which leads to more distrust. It becomes a self-fulfilling prophecy, really. Where you used to trust them to have your best interests at heart, it's different now. Perhaps you ignored the warning signs as they cropped up, certain that your friend would never cause you harm. Part of the recovery process, and an essential element in reducing your stress and the drama of it all, is grieving the friendship and taking a fearless inventory of how you might have paid closer attention. Remember: Never trust a dog to watch your sandwich. Business has no room for wishful thinking. If they have been irresponsible in the past, don't expect a 180 degree change. Expect more of the same and behave accordingly.

That last entrepreneur spent a great deal of time in denial and then in "fix-it" mode and he paid the price, dearly. He kept trying to make something work that was bound for failure. As a result, he suffered more, as did the business.

Fighting and resisting things that are blocking you saps your energy and passion. It tactic prevents you from moving forward because you're literally stopping on your path to *move* things that you could *go around*. What a waste! Take space, get some perspective, shut the world out for a few hours or a day if you have to so that you can collect your thoughts. If nasty texts or emails are sailing around, shut off the electronic devices that are aggravating the drama. They feed into the perpetuation of the drama. Take space. Give yourself distance. Get perspective. And unravel your mess before it takes you down with it.

"Peace is the result of retraining your mind to process life as it is, rather than as you think it should be." ~ Dr. Wayne W. Dyer

~ Keys to the Cage ~

What's at the root of all of these problems? Ineffective communication, conflict, and perception challenges. As I wrote about in **Feed The Need**, it's human nature to answer our drive to meet our core needs (control, connection, purpose, validation). Issues (and conflicts, dramas, and stress) arise when we:

- Aren't getting them met.
- Try to get them met in the wrong ways, at inopportune times, with the wrong people.
- Don't recognize the needs drive in others, leaving them unsatisfied.

Let's tackle these one at a time, shall we?

When we aren't getting our core needs met, we get frustrated, anxious, angry, depressed, resentful, and a whole host of other negative things.

If you want to feel engaged (yes, that's a work way of saying "connection"), you need to have a clear sense of the mission of the organization you're working for. This ties directly into feeling like you're working with purpose (where and how you're going) and validation (demonstration that you're valued). If your company puts their mission front and center, you might be surprised to hear that more companies than not do a lousy job of getting their employees behind their mission. Case in point, I was conducting a seminar for a leadership team recently and I asked them to tell me their mission so we could prepare for a discussion about engagement. They looked at me like I had three heads. A few piped up that their mission was to make money off of their customers. The head executive in the room was flabbergasted (and ticked off), shocked that none of these people could articulate the company's mission. Even worse, the head executive shared with me afterward that the mission had *just* been communicated the week prior in a company mass communication. Let me just add that part of the problem was that the mission was long, convoluted, and evoked no emotion (except boredom) from anyone reading it. Please don't get me started on the efficacy of mass communications.

Too late. I have to take a moment to explore this highly-trusted approach.

Please don't misunderstand my sarcasm. Mass communications have their place in the communication hierarchy. They are helpful to get word out to everyone in a fast manner. The issue is that, too often, company executives stop there. "We told them! We sent an email!" Okay, well, yes, you did. Bravo! If checking the box is all you wanted to accomplish then I'll award you a gold star for your efforts. If you want your employees engaged, feeling connected to your initiative, to the mission of the company, then you'd best keep going. I've heard other executives tout that they did the mass communication *and* they put up *signs around the office*. Again, bravo! You took a valiant step toward having an engaged workforce!

It's still not enough. It's been said that you need to repeat an idea to a person seven times before they hear it enough to repeat it. Others say it's more like 50 times. Fifty times?! That's a lot of mass emails and signs! I'm kidding. It's so much more complicated than that. It's not about spoon feeding people a message over and over again. Mass emails, signs, or any other message-repetition system together aren't enough. If you want people to feel engaged in your mission or program, you need to involve them in it. You need the words to come out of their mouths not just go into their ears.

Let me say that again. The message needs to come out of their mouths not just into their ears. We spend so much time saying things over and over again, thinking that eventually it'll "get through." If you've had success doing this then by all means, please don't let me stop you! Most of us, however, slam up against a brick wall when we try to "get through." You've probably heard the old adage, "teaching is the best teacher." When you are responsible for imparting information to others, you learn a lot in the process. If you want people to internalize the message you're sharing, put them in charge of sharing it with others.

"Just for the record, darling, not all positive change
feels positive in the beginning." ~ S. C. Lourie

Example

The companies I partner with to create cultural change often contact me after they've tried this "get through" method. They've spent an inordinate amount of time deciding what needs to change culturally, sent their senior management out with the agenda for change, and created messaging to deliver the news. Check. Check. Check! So, why the need for Dr. B.? Easy. They forgot to involve the masses. Of course, when I asked them if they'd involved the masses already, they were quick to answer, "yes!" Lies. They "involved" them by "telling" them.

That's not involvement. That's transmitting. These highly intelligent and incredibly motivated leaders got excited and jumped into implementation before getting all layers of the organization to get invested in it. Kudos to them for even getting started and mad props to them for calling me in, of course! How did I fix these situations? Each one was slightly different but the core shift was the same: I pulled in the masses and put them in charge of implementing the change, often through committee representation (implementation teams).

What did this accomplish? It got the people who needed to be part of the change to be the spokespeople for it and put them in control of it by doing the heavy lifting and advising senior leadership. The people on the ground became the ones with the message coming *out of their mouths*, not just receiving it *in their ears*. They were engaged, involved, and in charge. They removed the "us vs. them" stalemate. They became part of the solution which made all of the difference.

If you want to feel connected to your colleagues or your boss and you keep getting the cold shoulder every time you reach out, over time you're likely to disengage from the work and from the company. If your work relationships are characterized by backstabbing politics, high school drama antics, and stress-producing exchanges, you're apt to get sucked into all of it if you stay long enough. Positive engagement has been shown to produce higher levels of productivity, creativity, and profitability so anything that reduces or removes that should be safeguarded against. Engagement is facilitated by people feeling that their work, the company, has a purpose. By validating their role in the company and stressing the importance of their contributions. There's the story about the janitor at NASA was asked what his job was and he replied, "to put a man on the moon." If you can inspire that kind of response from the people in your organization, you may just put a person on another celestial being. When people are engaged, they also feel more in control and vice versa because of that handy little phenomenon of self-determination, of feeling instrumental in your own fate.

If we can change our behavior and everything around us could change, how great would that be? We live in a heliocentric solar system (unless you're part of that new society that asserts differently and thinks there is an advanced society that lives in Earth's core, accessible through a hole at the North Pole, but I digress). For countless years, Earthlings thought we were geocentric, with all the planets and the sun revolving around US.

Somewhere along the way we've become Me-centric. If someone has a snarky look on their face when they meet with us, we are inclined to think, "how dare you look at me like that?" It would be far more helpful to our mental health, not to mention our relationships, to wonder, "what might have happened to put that look on her face?" You can certainly ponder what the look on their face may have to do with your relationship, but getting stuck on that thought track doesn't allow for other perspectives to be considered.

"The worst bullies you will ever encounter in your life are your own thoughts." ~ Bryant McGill

People personalize everything. When someone behaves badly, we often do one of two things: we think it's a personal affront against us or we blame it entirely on the other person.

~ Control Conundrum ~

Just like everything in life, it's more complicated than that. But don't lose hope: It can be seen quite simply. It's what I call the

Control Conundrum. We think we are more or less in control than we really are and that affects our thoughts, feelings, and behaviors. What makes it a conundrum is that we say we want to be in control, we know it would allow us to feel better, yet we hand over our control to the very person/people we don't trust. We hand over our power because we don't take stock and responsibility over the following statement:

We are each responsible for our own thoughts, feelings, and behaviors. That means that other people are each responsible for their own thoughts, feelings, and behaviors. I used to call this the Control Buckets.

When we fly off the handle saying, "she made me so mad that I xyz," we are making the other person responsible for our thoughts, feelings, and behaviors. In effect, we are *handing over our control.* We are allowing our train of thought to be hijacked by someone else. And usually not a special someone else; often by an inconsequential jerk. Am I right? Have you been down that ugly road? Maybe you're on it right this very minute, letting some angry, pained, broken person call the shots in YOUR head. Why? For the love of all things good, WHY? Of all people to let take up space in your head and to inform your next feeling or action…THEM? No, no, no. Not now. Not when you have today to spend in any way you choose. Why would you choose that?

I'll tell you why. Because most of us were raised to believe that someone else (or the world at large) was in charge of us. That the things that other people said or did could have some immense effect on our lives. Usually, because they DID. Why? Because we LET THEM. Regardless of who they were or how much they had to say about you or your life, they were never in control of how you thought, felt, or behaved. Never. Not even for a second. You simply handed over the control, probably without even thinking of it.

Exercise: Power of a Penny

Get a penny, preferably a beautiful, clean, and shiny penny. Hold it in your hand and close your eyes. Feel the strength and durability of that penny. Since you know that your feelings and behaviors emanate from your thoughts, imagine that this penny represents your thoughts. And, in your thoughts lies your *power*. Your influence in the world. Your experience of everything and everyone around you. Would you hand that precious penny over to anyone? Would you hand that powerful coin over to some jerk who has no business holing your most precious possession? Of course you wouldn't. Carry this penny in your pocket for the next week (longer is better!) and every time you feel yourself getting aggravated by someone or getting your head all wrapped up in someone else's words or actions, stop. Center yourself on making thoughtful connection with your penny. Hold it firmly in your grasp and make a commitment not to hand it over to anyone by letting their words or actions be in charge of yours. Your power is in that penny. Don't let someone else spend it for you.

"One's dignity may be assaulted, vandalized, and cruelly mocked,
but it can never be taken away
unless it's surrendered." ~ Michael J. Fox

~ Invested Detachment ~

At the root of so much unrest is making internal what can be left external. It's pretty basic and reminds me of something that was bandied around on the playground when we were kids: "Sticks and stones may break my bones but words will never hurt me." We heard it, but do we LIVE by it? Most people and teams that I coach struggle the most because they internalize the words of others without even pausing. The words are said and they become a part of the person hearing them almost immediately.

Sometimes it's not even words, but mere inferences. Someone slights them in a meeting and before the room is emptied, the affected staff member is churning on the inside, often already plotting their revenge. It happens every single day in Corporate America. Slights, even perceived ones, are committed throughout the day and it's decided that someone has to pay for them. Sometimes the "punishment" is having others turned against them through the rumor mill, coffeemaker-side chatter, and eye rolling indicating they the "offender" is disapproved of. Other times it's more focused with passive-aggressive actions that give the "offender" the cold shoulder through response delays or "mistakes" or "oversights," often excluding them or their influence from key discussions and decisions.

> "Let go of the people who dull your shine,
> poison your spirit, and bring you drama.
> Cancel your subscription to their issues." ~ Steve Maraboli

~ Emotional Ladder ~

Imagine you're doing some work on your house using a ladder. You've asked a neighbor to stay at the bottom of the ladder to keep it steady. Let's suppose you both start climbing at the same time, what happens to you both? You both come crashing down. If you climb down while they are climbing up, who is in control? You. You're not only in control of your own contribution to the situation, you're perceivably in control of the situation itself.

I've had countless conversations with clients about what makes a person a good and effective leader. If you consider a leader in their most basic form, they are out in front. When we were in elementary school, there were the line leaders who led us from activity to activity. A leader leads us into something and away from something else. In order to attract and sustain true followers (versus those who follow out of desperation or necessity), the leader requires one thing above all else: Trust. Followers must offer their trust to a leader in order to create a strong followership.

At the core of trust is safety. We demand to feel safe at some level before we will offer our trust. Think about what feeling safe is like for you. What qualities do people have who you trust to lead you? Who are the people who you feel more immediate trust for versus those who make you uncomfortable in a leadership capacity?

How I describe people who I find trustworthy to lead me?

If I were a betting woman, I'd guess that somewhere in that description were words like:

- Strong
- Even-tempered
- Fair
- Reliable
- Consistent

When we can rely on something we are more apt to trust it. Trust means loosening the reigns on our control efforts. When we trust something we don't feel obliged to exert control over it. We can let go a little bit and focus on others things. Conversely, if we don't trust someone or something, we often end up expending a great deal of effort trying to head off things at the pass, trying to get in front of events before they go the wrong way.

If anyone has ever been in a relationship with an addict, it's a lot like that. You know they aren't trustworthy so you try to figure out how to stay two steps ahead of them. You calculate their next move so you can not only anticipate it and mentally prepare yourself, but also try to minimize the fallout. On the job, if you don't trust your leader, you're likely to work twice as hard trying to cover your ass at every turn, cover up mistakes, and do damage control whenever possible. It's downright exhausting. And wasteful. It wastes your time, attention, and talent on trying to control someone else's actions, which, by definition, is insanity. You can't control anyone else, only you.

> "Our best decisions are often what we choose
> not to get involved in." ~ Doug Cooper

~ Dialing Down the Drama ~

Brag moment: My clients absolutely love this next one!

We are routinely greeted with invitations to engage in dramas at work. There are days that person after person you run into at work seem hell-bent on infuriating you, goading you into their drama. They say inciting things to stir you up, either in an effort to oppose you or to team up with you against a common enemy. I call these workplace players the *clowns*. Their job is to engage you whether you like it or not. They want to get a reaction because that's how they gather their power, by robbing you of yours. Ever see someone at the circus who doesn't like clowns (and who DOES?) get approached by one? You can watch the person go from calm, cool, and collected to an abrasive jerk in 0.2 seconds with a clown up in their face.

If you were to take a before and after reading of the target's blood pressure, you'd find a sizeable difference pre- and post-clown. Their chest may feel tight, their fists may be clenched, and they may feel a stirring in their stomach. When your body starts to respond like this to the actions of others it's a surefire sign that you're about to react emotionally to whatever is happening around you. I call it the "throat to pelvis" indicator system.

If you feel something between your throat and your pelvis (granted, some of you will feel it in your jaw, so let's include that, too) when you read an email or are in a meeting or on a call, it's time to slow your roll down and be diligent with your response. Your body is telling you what your mind might be slow to reveal: You're being triggered and you're likely to react in a way that probably won't serve you in the long run. It's like the warning light system in your vehicle: It's your body yelling to you to pull over, take stock, and fix something before the whole system fails and costs you a boatload of money.

Responding from emotion may feel good in the moment but it doesn't serve you (or reduce drama) in the long-run. Responding from emotion is the center stage act under the big top circus that is the modern workplace. If everyone at the office would take a moment to check into their indicator system, collect themselves, and respond instead of react, the workplace would quickly lose its circus status. If a few people would do it, it would necessarily get better because you'd be adding ringleaders and losing clowns. It's a sheer numbers and influence thing.

Drama is all about distance, or the lack thereof. Drama is cultivated when people respond to situations with their guts instead of their heads. When you react instead of responding. What do I mean by that? Reacting is a swift movement toward a stimulus without space or distance from it. Responding is a slow and deliberate approach to a problem. The difference? Distance. Thoughtfulness. Intention. Consideration of the outcome. Practicing this sort of mindfulness at work is incredibly empowering.

It's by developing what I like to call Emotional Agility.

What is Emotional Agility anyway? Emotional Agility is based on the Agility Matrix.

The Agility Matrix illustrates how

thoughts, feelings, and behaviors are

influenced by and influence circumstances and choices.

~ Agility Matrix ~

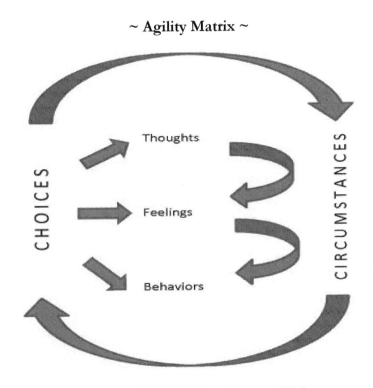

Property of Dr. Bridget Cooper, 2015

When I was in school, it drove me nuts when I'd see a diagram and then below it was a page of text trying to explain it to me in some complicated fashion. It made me feel like I was expected to channel Aristotle or Einstein through some space-time continuum. Lucky for you, I'm not going to torment you that way, at least not on this page. Below is the nitty gritty of the model, in easy-to-read bullet form. The pathway looks like this:

- We make choices about how to think about things.

- Our thoughts about things lead to our feelings about things.

- Our feelings about things lead to how we behave in response to things.

- How we behave leads to a host of circumstances in our lives.

- Those circumstances then influence the choices we have open to us and the ones we make.

The matrix feeds backwards, as well:

- The circumstances in our lives affect how we think about things.

- How we think about those circumstances in our lives affects our feelings.

- Those feelings affect our behavior.

- Our thoughts, feelings, and behavior then affects the choices we make about things in our lives.

Awareness requires presence, presence requires focus, and focus requires calm. The good news? This kind of calm is powerful. With calm, you can exercise a wider range of choice and **those with more *choice* have more *power.***

Three things that you need to know about the Agility Matrix:

1. The Agility Matrix is neither voodoo nor rocket science.
2. The Agility Matrix amounts to control that is exercised in healthy and productive ways.
3. The Agility Matrix is built on intuitive thinking, about how things come to be in our lives.

Now that you know what your intended outcome is – to enhance your emotional agility – it's time to continue to collect the resources to support your change journey by assessing what's going on outside of you.

Recognize that you have 360 degrees of options. That's an amazing number of choices, most of which you've never even considered. I can't tell you how many people come to me and tell me that they "have" to do such and such or they "have no choice." Bull. There is an entire sea full of options in front of you, every minute of every day. The more agile you are, the more options you can *see* and *employ*. Emotional agility is demonstrated by embracing and enacting choice over thoughts, feelings, and actions. Your degree of Emotional Agility is measured by the *ease* and *flexibility* of embracing and enacting that choice. Emotional Agility is change in and of itself: It allows for it by its nature. In other words, it's being flexible.

The hallmarks of Emotional Agility are:

1. **Insight** – Understanding people and oneself, seeing motivations, aware of stuff beyond the "chatter" or "noise" of what the problem may look like on the outside.

2. **Distance-ability** – Decreasing emotional and reactive response by being able to create distance and perspective about the situation.

3. **Flexibility** – Thinking and behaving differently in response to internal and external cues.

How do you know when you have a high degree of *insight?* You'll be able to focus on the thoughts, feelings, and actions of others and not just your own. You'll be inclined to look first at the motivations behind a person's behavior instead of "they did such and such." Most importantly, your focus will be on understanding the problem instead of jumping to conclusions that lead you straight to blame others.

How do you know when you're a pro at *distance-ability?* You won't react to the behavior of others without thinking it through first. You'll tend to be calm, even in the most reactive and volatile situations. You'll be able to observe how the situation <u>wants</u> you to feel, but you won't fall into that trap without calculating the consequences.

How do you know when you're mastering *flexibility?* You'll note that you have a variety of options in any given situation. You recognize that even though you might instinctively want to act in a certain way, you *do* have other options you can consider. You observe internal and external cues that might affect the way you think and behave and use these cues to make decisions about how to respond.

What does Flexibility look like in real-life situations? People with Flexibility don't automatically do things just because they did it that way before. If someone sits in their seat, they move to another seat. If plans change, they adapt to the new ones. When they are faced with a dilemma, they think through their options. They brainstorm. They don't react, they respond thoughtfully. They are good at pausing so that they can see the choices available. When it seems that they only have one choice, they investigate and challenge to unearth more choices. They aren't affixed to one solution, they entertain many possible solutions. They favor effectiveness over efficiency.

"When we recognize that we have a habit of replaying old events and reacting to new events as if they were the old ones, we can begin to notice when that habit energy comes up. We can then gently remind ourselves that we have another choice. We can look at the moment as it is, a fresh moment, and leave the past for a time when we can look at it compassionately." ~ Thich Nhat Hanh

It took an emotionally agile boss not to fly off the handle and call their employee to task when faced with this humdinger.

Sending a note: Think about the recipient. I know this sounds like kindergarten wisdom but you'd be surprised at how often it's overlooked. One of my clients had the following text conversation from one of his employees about a valued colleague.

> Employee: I have some news about Betty.
>
> Boss: What happened?
>
> Employee: She got in a car accident. Rear-ended at a stop sign.
>
> Boss: Is she okay? When? How did you find out?
>
> Ten minutes pass...
>
> Employee: Over the weekend. She's fine, just some neck pain. Her car needs repairs.

Imagine for a moment being this boss. During that ten minute gap, what terrible thoughts are going through my client's head? That Betty is on life support? Suffered irreversible brain damage? All sorts of panic-laden thoughts are going through his head as he waits, very impatiently, for a response from his employee. When my client shared this exchange with me I immediately questioned if this employee was a person who had a high need for control (over information, needing to be "in the know") and a penchant for drama (wanting to stir the proverbial pot to evoke an emotional response in her boss, which is another form of control).

What's the lesson here? Imagine *being in the recipient's shoes* when you send out communication. If this employee had paused and thought through this, she would have started off with news of the accident, flowing quickly in to the report that Betty was fine (or vice versa). Being intentional about communication, considering the message you're sending and why, starves the drama in any situation.

There's a certain acceptance in responding. You're invited to accept that things may not be at all affected by your response to the situation; that you are but a cog in a very large, complicated wheel. You are accepting a lack of control. You're acting upon a situation, speaking up, but knowing that it may or may not matter. When you react, you're on autopilot. You're operating under an unspoken, and often subconscious, thought that when you speak or act in a certain way that it'll keep something under your control.

"The quieter you become,
the more you are able to hear." ~ Rumi

In my household, the faster you spoke, the better. Having smart, witty retorts was expected. I always felt compelled to be in front of anything and everything. I was on constant alert at all times. Watching, listening, scanning my environment for the next opportunity to try to fix or confront or avoid something. Growing up in an addicted family system is replete with chances to jump in and rescue anything and everything before anyone even has a chance to breathe let alone think. It's like you're fighting to get life into slow motion, except for you, so you have a snowball's chance in fixing something before it blows up before your eyes.

Drama feeds on people who come from the place I come from. Feeds on it. It's like a Thanksgiving feast for the drama gods when someone like me walks in the door. I fight it hard, and I mean HARD, when I see something or someone that needs fixing or a conversation. It's a compulsion to intervene. Compulsions operate at the subconscious level so you're not really thinking through anything before you act. If you do think, the automatic thoughts are consistent with what your compulsions are instructing you to do, so you don't question the compulsion. Want an example?

John has a compulsion to correct people when they do something wrong. John is in a meeting at work and one of his peers walked in late, yet again. As they make their way to the table, disrupting the meeting that's already in session, John rolls his eyes. He thinks to himself, "what a disruptive, disrespectful jerk. I should say something. But I won't, I'll be good. I'm totally justified in rolling my eyes. So what if anyone saw me? Everyone knows how much of a pain in the butt that person is. Who would blame me?"

Think again. Here's the Drama Doctor to diagnose this situation. Let me share a few questions I'd ask.

- What happens next? After the eye rolling?
- Who is involved in this situation?
- What can you do to influence whether or not your co-worker is on time, directly with your co-worker?
- What can you do to influence tardiness with your co-workers across the board?

~ Summary ~

Taking part in dialing down the drama in your office will pay off in spades, especially if you are in a leadership position. You have the ability to influence others. This chapter offered a number of tactics and lenses to employ to reclaim your personal power in the circus, to hold your own whip. That's the point of the book, people: To offer you ways to reclaim your power because why wouldn't you want that?

Key Chapter Concepts

- Drama is dashed by using the "throat to pelvis" awareness approach.
- When you're not getting your needs met, drama often ensues.
- Invested detachment can help to remove the ego from conversations, dialing down the drama.
- Using the Emotional Ladder approach will help you to reduce conflict.
- Emotional Agility will help you keep drama at bay.

"When faced with senseless drama, spiteful criticisms, and misguided opinions, walking away is the best way to stand up for yourself. To respond with anger is an endorsement of their attitude." ~ Dodinsky

6

TIGER'S DEN

"If you know your enemy and yourself then
every battle is won." ~ Park Tae Seo

~ Isolation and Connection ~

Isolation flies in the face of connection. The informal hallway conversation is impossible when people aren't even in the same time zone. We've sacrificed convenience for connection. Often the marketplace demands the outsourcing occurs or work-from-home relationships are negotiated. Believe it or not, there are some regions of the country that struggle to locate qualified individuals so their desperation leads to entertaining long-distance work relationships in order to source talent.

People are isolated through truncated social connections. Some organizations take stock of the disconnection and seek to pool their departments so that people can interact more casually and regularly without the distance barrier. From experience, this is often met with resistance by employees who have been conditioned to work independently and without disruption. Suddenly, they are thrust into noisy, open cubicle environments with frequent disruptions and distractions.

So what does this say about geographic isolation? Is it good or is it bad? It's both. Like with all things, there's an upside and a downside. People, particularly introverts and those who have jobs that require a high degree of focus and extended periods of concentration do best when they are not in an overly social, interactive environment. Conversely, the team may suffer if those same individuals are overly secluded.

What's the solution for teams that are able to be placed together but it's possible that you won't reap the benefits of their productivity and loyalty if you do? Compromise. Some concessions might include:

- Taller cubicle walls.
- Noise baffles (extract the disruptive, environmental sound).
- Permitting earbuds or headphones.
- Collaboration rooms so that impromptu meetings are held away from other workers who are trying to focus.
- Focus rooms for quiet work when employees can bring their work, laptops, etc. to get out of the more hectic environment.

In the workplace, people are often at a loss as to how to manage conflict. They routinely fear being confrontational in case the other party complains about them and accuses them of harassment. Instead, they shut the person out emotionally and create an experience of isolation. The interesting thing is that intentional isolation is, in and of itself, a form of bullying, of social control and intimidation. People are social creatures, whether they are introverted or extroverted. As human beings we have four core needs – *control,* *connection, purpose,* and *validation* – that need to be fulfilled or we will seek to fill them in dysfunctional and destructive ways. If an employee is being isolated you can imagine that their need for connection isn't being met. In order to calm that inner storm and lack of fulfillment, they may act out (anger, disruption, dramatic behavior) or act "in" (directing their angst toward themselves in the form of depression, anxiety, stress-related illness, or searching for a new job).

Example

Marie was an experienced administrative professional who took a job that perfectly suited her abilities. She's a social person and thrives on a team. Unfortunately, from a social standpoint, her teammates were harsh, snappy, and happy to be solo. From a professional standpoint, they were downright incompetent and made errors more often than most people take breaths. She was aggravated and they could sense it. Since collaboration was a priority for her, she focused on trying to connect with her co-workers. The more she challenged their comfort zones socially, the more they cast her out. She kept thinking if she just tried a little harder she could get them to work as a team and improve the quality of their work, as well as the work experience. No luck there. They ostracized her which eventually made it hard for her to get her work done. She stayed at the job for far too long, suffering severe emotional and physical issues due to the rejection. This took her years to recover from.

All of these behaviors negatively affect the organizations these people work for. They create a lack of health in the culture and promote stress and drama, in addition to the social isolation. They all go hand in hand and create a "chicken or the egg" phenomenon. Did the stress and drama lead to the isolation or the other way around.

It's no small wonder that executives are confused as to how and where to intervene to affect and change it for the better.

"Isolation is the worst possible counselor." ~ Miguel de Unamuno

Before we can solve isolation, we first have to finish analyzing it to make certain that we fully understand it. Next up: An investigation of one of our most favorite social labels: Introverts vs. Extroverts.

~ Introverts vs. Extroverts ~

A common discussion I tackle with clients is the identification of introverts and extroverts and how those definitions interface with office dynamics. The introvert movement is gaining a lot of momentum, in part because our society has often spoken about introverts as being broken somehow. As a self-proclaimed extrovert, I stand with the self-proclaimed introverts and proclaim that nothing is further from the truth. Both groups are simply a set of dispositions and preferences, not good or bad. There's also a great deal of confusion of what "introvert" and "extrovert" actually mean. "Introvert" is often interchanged with "shy" or "lacking confidence" while "extrovert" is used synonymously with "outgoing" and "confident." Here are some facts about extroversion and introversion:

- These terms refer to how: 1) people draw energy from the environment and, 2) process information.
- Introverts draw energy from solitude and feel sapped of it in group (especially in large group) situations. Extroverts draw energy from groups and get stir crazy when they have too much solitude.

- Introverts need time to reflect to give you responses; they prefer to think through things ahead of time to be able to process their thoughts and opinions. Extroverts can offer opinions and thoughts off the cuff without much hesitation.

- It's been said that no one is either 100% introverted or 100% extroverted; that anyone who is completely introverted or extroverted would be psychotic. It's a spectrum and there's a new identifier called an "ambivert" which is the blend of the two.

- Companies benefit from both types. For instance, introverts are less likely to make agreements without due diligence whereas extroverts are likely to forge relationships easier.

- Both introverts and extroverts need accommodations to do their best work. Extroverts need frequent collaboration with others because they enjoy and get energized by interaction. Introverts need alone time to concentrate and organize their thoughts.

If you're working with an extrovert, hallway conversations and group meetings solicit good information and invigorate their thinking. If you're working with an introvert, providing them time to ponder something yields the best results.

If you're managing an extrovert, you'll see them flourish in a bullpen-type office environment, not necessarily by giving them a secluded corner office unless it's inviting to others to collaborate in it. If you're managing an introvert, you'll need to provide taller cubicle walls, earbuds, and perhaps a "workroom" with a door if you want to bring out their best work and attitude.

To summarize, physical isolation is a matter of degrees and preference to some extent. Your extroverts are much more sensitive to feeling the effects of isolation, and may perceive that condition whereas an introvert might not be phased by it. Knowing and communicating with people is critical to ensuring that people are able to give their level best to their organization, with physical environment being a key factor to productivity and engagement.

What does all of this have to do with taming the work circus? Plenty. We've examined the four core human needs that drive our behavior: **control**, **connection**, **purpose**, and **validation**. We've observed what happens when one or more of those needs aren't being fulfilled: people act out, usually disruptively, often without even being able to name which need they are seeking to meet. They are unhappy and unhappy people are inherently less productive, engaged, and successful.

When it comes to introverts and extroverts and giving them the environment they need to work optimally, how they get their needs met has to be a considerable factor. Putting them in charge of as much of the decision as possible is a start. This is not to advocate that you let the monkeys run the circus; it's simply to remember that people want to be in control so if you don't give up a little, somehow, some way, there will be negative repercussions. At the very least, their lack of control needs to be acknowledged and empathized with before you can expect people to move on. If you're on the receiving end of things, be alert to your inherent need to be in control of things and work to define:

- What you can control, or request to control?
- What you can influence, or request to influence?
- What you have no control or influence over and need to let go of?

Are you experiencing one of those "not in my control" moments at work right now? Take a moment and ponder it, using this framework. Use the space below to write about it.

First, what's the situation? Briefly describe what the problem is.

What can I control?

What can I request to control (ask to be put in charge of advocating, deciding, implementing, communicating)?

What can I influence?

What can I request to influence (ask to be a part of advocating, deciding, implementing, and communicating)?

What do I have no opportunity to control or influence and need to let go of?

Now that we've investigated your situation, let's take a look at another real-life situation.

Case Study: I worked with a company that was looking for more collaboration among its employees so it sought to solve that by pulling all of their engineers (known introverts) into a cubicle environment in what can best be described as an airplane hangar. Noisy and distracting didn't begin to cover it. The few engineers and support people who were more extroverted were thrilled with the opportunity to collaborate and seek frequent input from their colleagues. The introverted ones, well, not so much. They were downright horrified by the constant interruptions, disruptions, and distractions. To make matters worse, management had neglected a very critical step in the implementation process: Telling the affected persons that it was happening! Yeah, they did that. Or, rather, they *didn't* do that.

Basically, employees were told one morning, "hey, so, we are moving to the cubicles out on the floor today. Boxes are available in the hall for you to pack your stuff. Find your name on a wall to find your spot. See you out there!"

I wish I was kidding. I wish I could tell you that this has never happened anywhere before or since, but I can't. This actually happens! Why? I boil it down to one really simple, critically-missed step: Communication, or the lack thereof. Why? A gap in skills. The unwillingness to tackle tough conversations and deliver bad news. So what do they do? They avoid communication until a crisis point is hit. By that point, the proverbial shit hits the fan: People are caught off guard, there's no preparation, and our instinct is to react to sudden shifts with emotion, usually of a negative variety.

Imagine being one of those engineers? How mad would you be? If you had a trusting, collaborative, respectful relationship with management you'd probably still be pretty irritated because you were jarred and had little time to adapt. More likely, your relationship with management has had rocky points and trust isn't the highest it could be. In that case, the lack of communication and last minute announcement probably felt like confirmation of every negative perception you ever had of the powers that be. The long-term effects of that are difficult to quantify but, rest assured, they are immense. Immediately, it's a huge stressor.

Since stress is the difference between that which you can control and that which you seek to control, a blindsiding like this creates a huge gap between those two states. You're moving your office whether you like it or not. You hardly have time to put up a fight, and zero time to influence the decision since it's already been made. Stress is off the charts for most people confronted in this manner. They feel disrespected, victimized, and undervalued.

Now let's take a moment to think about the range of reactions that followed this office move ambush. Suffice it to say that the affected group reacted, and generally not in productive ways. Because they had no preparation and no input, they resorted to passive-aggressive means to make their disgust clear. Their productivity suffered, as a sort of self-fulfilling prophecy, blamed on the new environment. They started being late and unprepared to meetings, citing the "chaos" of the new environment. They made more errors, missed more deadlines, and so on. The cubicle-side conversations undermined management and reinforced an "us vs. them" mentality.

If you're ever put in this type of situation, consider these questions.

How do you solve isolation if you're the isolated one?

How do you solve isolation if you're in leadership?

How do you assess what's functional vs. dysfunctional isolation?

The point of all of these questions is to point you toward claiming your power in any situation. In recognizing where you have control and where you don't. In seeing where you have influence and where you don't. As a leader, it reminds you of the importance of considering control when making decisions. Leaders can also feel isolated. As one new manager shared, leading people calls in all sorts of new dilemmas.

Even though they are for health-related issues, co-worker absences can leave a strain on the remaining workers and stress and drama can occur. "Do they really have a doctor's appointment? Do they need to take the whole day?" These are some of the comments I receive and frankly sometimes feel. For me as a director I struggle with having compassion and ensuring that the work gets done. I have seen many positive actions from employees during these occasions and for the most part great teamwork. We have all grown from these experiences. However, when I dreamed of advancing my career to eventually becoming the "boss" I had no idea of the mix of emotions I would have managing staff. I guess that would be the emotional isolation I often feel. I always have to take the high road and make decisions that I'm not always confident about or feel equipped to make.

Another employee shares how important good leadership is in mitigating the feeling of isolation.

My job was extremely isolating and the majority of feedback came from one very negative, dysfunctional person. What helped me to succeed was getting out and networking with others in healthy and high-functioning situations. Seeing how things are done in a healthy and supportive way gave me strength to focus and get through my difficult situation. Unfortunately, I did not do this nearly often enough. The ultimate solution came when the person got a new job, left, and I began working with someone new who was very competent and supportive.

Make no mistake about people: If you take their control away they will find a way to recapture and assert it.

~ Summary ~

As you know from earlier chapters, the triple threat of stress, drama, and isolation are connected and have some pretty significant overlaps. We addressed bullying in the stress chapter, but you can easily see how behavior that leads to isolation is bullying. In order to not be overly repetitive in this chapter, I'll refer you back to the stress chapter to review the effects of intentional isolation on the workforce. In a later chapter, we will dive more into isolation as it relates to engagement.

Key Chapter Concepts

- The core human need for connection can be thwarted by isolation and produce dysfunctional behavior.
- Isolation is experienced differently for different people, particularly introverts vs. extroverts.
- Finding the right mix of privacy vs. interaction needs to be a priority for leaders of an organization.

REMEMBER THE LOTUS FLOWER

Great people will always be mocked by those
Who feel smaller than them.
A lion does not flinch at laughter coming from a hyena.
A gorilla does not budge from a banana thrown at it by a monkey.
A nightingale does not stop singing its beautiful song
At the intrusion of an annoying woodpecker.
Whenever you should doubt your self-worth,
remember the lotus flower.
Even though it plunges to life from beneath the mud,
It does not allow the dirt that surrounds it
To affect its growth or beauty.
Be that lotus flower always.
Do not allow any negativity or ugliness
In your surroundings
Destroy your confidence,
Affect your growth,
Or make you question your self-worth.
It is very normal for one ugly weed
to not want to stand alone.
Remember this always.
If you were ugly,
Or just as small as they feel they are,
Then they would not feel so bitter and envious
Each and every time they are forced
To glance up at magnificently
Divine YOU. ~ Suzy Kasseem

WALKING THE TIGHTROPE

"You either get bitter or you get better. It's that simple.
You either take what has been dealt to you and allow it
to make you a better person, or you allow it to tear you down.
The choice does not belong to fate, it belongs to you." ~ Josh Shipp

~ Change Starts From Within ~

If I haven't made myself clear enough to this point, I believe that all change comes from within. We cannot force our will on others sufficiently to change them, at least not long term. We might get them to follow our lead under close supervision and for a short time, but if they aren't invested in the change, it won't last. Lasting change comes from within each of us. We can model things for others and have an influence (small or large) on them, and we are best suited to do that when we are centered and strong and full of resolve to maintain our good behavior.

If we want to avoid becoming a sideshow act or part of the three-ring circus, we have to take responsibility for our own contribution to the mayhem. We have a part in it, often larger than we've been owning up to. We are either part of the solution or part of the problem. We either feed the circus animals, or withhold attention. In order to have any positive influence on the work circus, we need to take inventory of what our contribution is to the experience and make a commitment to reduce or remove it that contribution.

In my third book, **Stuck U.**, I outlined the 5-step change process. It's relevant here, so let me introduce it. That way, you'll have a roadmap for owning your part of the circus elimination.

No time like the present to kick this off....

The five-step change process looks like this:

Step 1: Awareness
Step 2: Acceptance
Step 3: Assessment
Step 4: Action
Step 5: Adjustment

Since you can't change someone else, you have to focus on what you can do to control your contribution and how you can influence (not control) others. You're only in charge of you, yet you can influence others around you by setting an example of how to behave differently. This example setting is especially effective if you seem happier and calmer as a result of your new approach. If you are in a leadership position, your influence has an even greater reach. You can sponsor seminars, lead discussions, make pronouncements about a new way of thinking, and, perhaps handing out a guide book (like **Power Play**) to help them along (hint, hint).

Finding a new center…a new you…is a challenge and needs attention or you may slide back to the old ways. Systems and old habits are strong. When the circus at work is in town, it's difficult not to get sucked back in. The key to success is following the five-step change process so you have the strength, insight, and tactics to hold onto your resolution to step out of the three-ring circus.

~ Step 1: Awareness ~

Awareness is the first step in the change process. The good news for you is that by picking up this book, you're already knee-deep in it. You know there's a problem. You may just be starting to inventory what the issues are and how deep they run. Ask yourself some questions to kick that off:

How does the circus make itself evident to me?

What are people saying to me about their experience at work? What are the common sentiments when I ask people about their day?

You might have other questions that you're likely to ask, so I invite you to make some notes here to ensure that you've at least scratched the surface of what you have on your hands.

~ Step 2: Acceptance as a Power Play ~

The most essential part of the 5-step change process is Acceptance. You're probably wondering why? It's simple: Acceptance brings about change because acceptance leads you to peace of mind and peace of mind brings power and influence. With that power and influence, you can orchestrate internal and external change. Before you can set out to change anything effectively, you need to start with accepting things exactly as they are. You need to appreciate that things didn't get to this place overnight; they followed a predictable path to this point. Getting out of this place is like following the breadcrumb trail back out of the woods. There is one major benefit to the acceptance step: Power. It looks like this:

Acceptance ◀━━━▶ **Peace** ◀━━━▶ **Power/Influence**

The lack of peace we experience in life, at work, and in any conflict anywhere, is directly attributed to a resistance to accept it. We want to change it. We want things to be different. We want to be in control of a circumstance or an outcome. Want to know the mind bender?

*The only way we can **change things** effectively is to first accept things as they are. And,*
*The only way we can **come to peace** is to accept things as they are.*
Finally, the only way we can be in
*our **full power and influential nature** is to come to peace.*

Therefore, the path to change and the path to peace are one in the same: Acceptance.

How can this possibly be? We've been taught to rage against the storm! To use the sheer power of our will to make things different. We have been raised to believe that we can make anything happen if we study hard enough, work long enough, argue convincingly enough. That somehow success has to do with us being *enough*.

Presenting itself simultaneously, and in direct contradiction to that model, is the victim stance that is pervasive and swirls around us all the time. We are encouraged to blame politicians, leaders, our parents, corporations, and anyone else with perceived power, for our troubles. Claiming victim status is a far cry from acceptance. Acceptance is a calm, quiet energy. It mirrors peace. It is a reflection place, a space to gather our energy, resources, insight, and power. It is the most powerful position, contrary to popular practice.

How can that possibly be? Aren't peaceful people feeble? Isn't accepting things as they are the weak position? Isn't that the equivalent of rolling over and playing dead? Isn't that how people take advantage of you?

It's all a matter of interpretation. Perspective. Experience. Let's get to that. What has been *your* experience with power?

What does *power* mean to you?

When have you felt most powerful?

What does *peace* mean to you?

When have you felt most peaceful?

What does *acceptance* mean to you?

When have you had to practice acceptance?

By answering the above questions, what did you learn about yourself and your attitudes about power, peace, and acceptance? What more do you have to work on or wrestle with to shift your thinking?

"Water is fluid, soft, and yielding. But water will wear away rock, which is rigid and cannot yield. As a rule, whatever is fluid, soft, and yielding will overcome whatever is rigid and hard. This is another paradox: What is soft is strong." ~ Lao Tzu

The strangest and most amazing thing about that is that once we accept things as they are, and we experience the peace that arrives with that acceptance, we are then truly in a power position to influence things. Wow! Think about that. When we are in resistance (the inverse of acceptance), we spend our power and influence in trying to change things, but our power is squandered because we are trying to overpower others while they are trying to overpower us. There is plenty of carnage and expended energy, but it's typically futile because both sides are fighting each other instead of addressing the real issue.

Once we get to acceptance, we can see more clearly. We find more options, more pathways, to reach the desired outcome. We stop being fixated on winning. We see what we can control, what we can influence, and what we need to let be. We come from a place of power instead of panicked reaction. We are calm. We can be in control of ourselves, fully. We can be influential.

That, folks, is our power play.

Example

I was coaching an executive (let's call her Jane) who had lost her political capital in her role. Before I was called in, Jane had reached an incredible level of frustration with her colleagues which was bleeding through to the entire division. She had grown sick and tired of taking the lead on things but she wanted things to get accomplished. It seemed that every employee had gotten sucked into the drama between Jane and her three counterparts. There were factions, as every one of their direct reports took sides, some crossing reporting relationship lines. It was a hot mess, and more "mess" than "hot."

What did I do? I met with the staff and each of her counterparts separately to get their perspectives. I quickly learned that they all felt like they were constantly letting Jane down. No matter what they did, they felt judged harshly. Jane was telling everyone how "they" needed to take action but everyone was waiting for someone else to take action, so things literally came to a screeching halt. The day-to-day work got done, but improvements and efficiencies that had been discussed ad nauseum just floated in the air, suspended in time. Jane had been in "fight" mode for quite a while, trying to assert her power with her colleagues and they responded with resistance, resentment, and retraction.

In my work directly with Jane, I encouraged her to see her power in accepting things as they were: Her colleagues taking a back seat to her overt leadership. Instead of feeling let down by their passivity, she could accept it as their way of being. Once she was able to process that and really accept that, she saw an opening: For Jane to step fully into her own power and accept the unofficial role of team leader to drive the change that she was seeking. Her colleagues were happy to acquiesce to her influence, letting her take the lead on defining new initiatives for the division and carrying out the work that needed to be done.

Her **acceptance** led to **peace** (within Jane and in the department) which led her to step into her **power** and take a leadership role, filling that vacuum. The entire division benefitted because the drama was dialed down, teamwork could commence, and Jane stopped raging against the system and instead led from within it.

Ready for Step 3 of the change process? Of course you are!

"Detachment is not that you should own nothing,
but that nothing should own you." ~ Ali Ibn Abi Talib

~ Step 3: Assessment ~

This is the fact-finding step. This is the time you spend observing, inquiring, and documenting all the signs that you've got a circus on your hands. You analyze how it got to this point. You dig for answers as to what exactly is broken and what can be fixed. To assist you in tackling this discovery step, I've provided some key questions to answer as you assess your current state and the resources you can line up to assist you in the change process.

What are the things that you find yourself saying about the culture (your one-liners, go-to statements)?

What do you say about yourself and your capacity to do things differently? Have you tried change agendas before and failed? Do you think that you're not capable of living a less stress-filled, drama-laden, isolated professional life? Do you think things are unchangeable? Do you believe that you aren't powerful enough to shift anything? How much power do you believe that you have?

What do people expect from one another? For example, in circus-oriented cultures, people expect others to ignore their emails and meeting requests, back-stab them, and fail at their respective jobs. Are these statements true at your organization? What else would you add?

What do you have going for you that will promote positive change? Like, are people sick and tired of things? Do you have new leadership? Has there been a recent crisis that has harnessed the attention of employees and leadership that something needs to change? Have there been some key hires (or fires) that have brought a change of attitude?

What are the resisting forces to change? Who seems invested in having it stay like it is? How are people benefitting from the circus? Do they have power because of it? Think on this one. If you don't reconcile what the resisting factors to change are you've failed before you've begun.

The last area of assessment required in any successful change process is addressing your Inner Critic effectively. We all have one. For some of us, it's boisterous and deafening. For others of us, it's there to undermine us when we least expect it. In order to set you up for success, here's your chance to connect with your inner critic so you can reduce its hold over you.

"Start by doing what's necessary, then do what's possible, and suddenly you are doing the impossible." ~ St. Francis of Assisi

One-on-One With Your Inner Critic

Bottom line: You need to develop trust with your inner critic.

You have proven that pesky voice right before. It's just like anyone else you have a relationship with: If you say one thing ("I want such and such") and do another, you've shown it that it can't trust what you say. It trusts what you *do*. You have to rebuild trust. You can acknowledge where you want to be, but still appreciate where you are and how you got there. Don't bother disagreeing with your subconscious. Instead, validate it. It weakens its fight. Like a rubber band snapping you back, don't run from it or it's going to sting. You *walk* with it, reassuring it that you hear the doubts and how you are calming it. If you read my book, **Feed The Need**, you know that the fourth need – Validation – is core to our happiness and trusting relationships. In the case of your subconscious, instead of receiving it from the outside, you have to deliver it on the inside.

All of that "agreeing with your Inner Critic" sounds completely crazy, right? It flies in the face of everything we've been taught! You're supposed to keep "your eyes on the prize" and "the end in sight." Yeah, well, those are catchy anecdotes but they miss a critical, and almost always overlooked, step in the change process. Acceptance isn't just a new-age, positive-thinking popular fad; it's at the core of why your change efforts have crashed and burned in the past. Why? Lack of trust. What? What does a lack of trust have to do with change? So much! It's all rooted in that pesky little player called your subconscious.

Over time, we've all amassed a certain number of failures. We've wanted things for our lives that we haven't succeeded in attaining. Maybe we've tried and failed. Maybe our failure is in our lack of trying at all, avoiding failure altogether (or so we think). Perhaps it's that stubborn 5-10 (or 50) pounds of extra weight that we just can't seem to shake off. Or, it's our resolution to be on time to appointments. It could be our vow to stay on top of our finances and stay out of debt.

Whatever our failures may be, our subconscious has been keeping score. By "keeping score" I mean to the level of your favorite uncle who can recount the stats from every player on their favorite team (or the entire league) for the past 40 years. Our subconscious knows every stumble, every broken promise, and every negative thing we've said to ourselves along the way. We've said over and over that we've got to change, yet we don't. So what has our subconscious heard?

- You hate this aspect of yourself.
- You need to change, but..
- You don't change.
- You expect this aspect of yourself to continue.
- You talk a good game but you won't really change.

What negative messages has your subconscious been hearing all these years? What have you been telling yourself about *you*? What messages have you been hearing from other people that you haven't shut down? What changes have you been telling yourself that you must make happen? Take a few minutes and write them down here.

Now is as good a time as any to meet your monster.

Monster Under Your Bed

I know, I know, you're not six years old anymore. Of course you don't believe in monsters under your bed. Guess what? I don't believe you. I haven't yet met a person who doesn't have a monster (or an entire village of them) under their beds. Think I've lost my mind? Nope. You have at least one monster – one fear – that keeps you from doing something. The biggest problems with having a monster under your queen-sized bed is that you don't even know what it looks like. Does it have two horns or none? One eye or three? Is it furry or does it have scales? My recommendation: Make friends with it. Look at it. Monsters are much less scary in the light.

What does "bringing your monster into the light" mean, practically speaking? It means that you need to fully examine your *fear*. You must acknowledge that you have a fear monster holding you back from going after your dreams and realizing your potential.

One of my clients a few years back was treading water in his career. If anyone was stuck, it was this guy. When I probed to find out what was holding him back from taking the necessary steps to grow his business, he responded that he might fail and he didn't want to risk that. So, he circled the drain and consistently felt like he was falling short. Want to know what I told him? I told him, "you might be right. You might fail and lose it all." He was so appreciative! I'm kidding. Instead he said, "you're a terrible coach!" I chuckled because I knew where I was going with this. Curious?

It's pretty simple. If you try to man handle or wrestle down your demons, they usually win. They have a great deal of power. They've been in charge of you for years (decades, even). Think they'll just step aside because you read some inspiring coffee table book filled with "success" quotes? Please. They want to hold their position, in part because they want to keep you safe. There's safety in not taking risks or putting yourself out there. Instead of arguing with your monsters, acknowledge them. They have a point, don't they? You've proven them right repeatedly...right? Stop telling them they're wrong or they'll keep showing up to demonstrate that they are right. That you're a failure. That the world is a scary place. That risk is scary.

They're not wrong. Not completely, anyway, so acknowledge the voice. Agree with its experience then ask it permission to show it another way, to offer another possible outcome. Direct your attention to the monsters instead of denying their existence. When you introduce yourself to the monster hiding under your bed it becomes less scary. The fear of the unknown is demolished. And, *you* just claimed more of your personal power.

So, tell me (okay, tell *you*), what's *your* monster? What's your fear? What self-fulfilling prophecy do you need to kick to the curb? What do you need to acknowledge before you can let it go?

"Talk to yourself the way you'd talk to someone you love. Shush your inner bully. Be your own bestie." ~ Karen Salmonsohn

~ Step 4: Action ~

This step is the doing step. It's when you stop thinking and start acting. It has the mystery of either hanging you up or being jumped to far too quickly. What do I mean? Some people get to this step and stall because the work is too intimidating. Others jump to this step right off the bat because they want results fast. Neither approach works, trust me.

First and foremost, to have things change, you have to want them to change.

You have to be clear on the upside and downside to change and be committed to seeing it through. Big changes can, and do, come in baby steps. If you've got an uphill battle, stay with it. Changing your thoughts changes your feelings which opens up new behavior patterns, starting with setting good intentions. Just saying "or" after you make a statement transforms your life through flexible thinking. I call that technique "The Big Or." That's all it takes to bend your rigid thinking into something more malleable.

When your run into calcified people in your organization, try that technique with them. If they make a strong, negative statement, just subtly say, "or?" See how they respond. You may just have moved a mountain.

Along the way to the promise land, you may get tired and worn out. Hopeless even. Use these stress busters to move yourself through that.

1. Have self-compassion.

2. Remember the "Big Picture."

3. Rely on routines.

4. Take five (or ten) minutes to do something you find interesting.

5. Add *where* and *when* to your to-do list.

6. Use if-thens for positive self-talk.

7. See your work in terms of progress, not perfection

8. Think about the progress that you've already made.

9. Know whether optimism or defensive pessimism works for you.

~ Step 5: Adjustment ~

This step is the reflection step. It's when you look back after what you've accomplished and see what you might have done differently and what is left to do. It's the Monday morning quarterback of the executive suite. There are three things you may need to adjust: Your expectations; your thoughts, feelings, behaviors; and the targeted change itself. If there have been tough times and there are more ahead, this is the point at which you need to come to terms with the losses you've faced and decide if you want to press on or opt out. Learning from our mistakes is an essential part of any good change process. In the adjustment step you may decide to do something differently, stop doing something, or start doing something. It's the time to course correct for the best possible outcome. That's what it's all about, right?

~ Summary ~

Maybe one of the reasons that people don't change much is because they don't have a roadmap to do it? I've provided an overview of this map here (more information available in my third book, **Stuck U.**). Another challenge is that for those who have a sense of the steps involved in changing things from the inside-out, they underestimate or don't understand the Acceptance step. We tend to want to glaze right over it. Unfortunately, that doesn't work. My advice: Follow the five steps from start to finish. Be true to them. Work them so they'll work for you.

We've spent some time talking about power through acceptance so I think it's high time to dig a little deeper and talk about how to move from that sense of peace to a place of power and influence. What does that really look like? What's involved? How do

I get from that place of calm to a place of influence in my life and in my work? Well, I won't spoil it. Turn the page.

Key Chapter Concepts

- There is a 5-Step change process that will help you to navigate your ticket out of the circus: Awareness, Acceptance, Assessment, Action, Adjustment.
- Acceptance is the most important of the five steps.
- In order to raise your awareness you need to understand your Inner Critic and your (fear) Monster.

"There are those who will resent you
for not being confined by their limitations." ~ Wayne Gerard Trotman

DOG & PONY SHOW

"It takes as much energy to wish
as it does to plan." ~ Eleanor Roosevelt

~ Choice & Control Conundrum ~

According to Emotional Agility and the Agility Matrix, your choice in thoughts leads to your choice in emotions which leads to your choice in behaviors. Those behaviors then lead to your circumstances (making them better, worse, or the same). Your circumstances then offer a new set of choices over your thoughts, feelings, and behaviors. And around and around we go. It turns into a debate of which came first: your circumstances or your choices?

We could argue that all day long and bore down into a nature or nurture deliberation, too. At the end of the day, the thing that truly matters is that you get to intervene at any time, at any point in the process, with *choice* and *clarity*. Clarity over what, you ask? Clarity over what you have choice over and what you don't; what you can control and what you cannot. As in:

You *cannot* control whether or not
other people are stressed out.

You *can* control whether or not *YOU* are stressed out.

You *cannot* control whether or not *other people*
are engaged in drama-based behavior,
creating a three-ring circus in the workplace.

You *can* control whether or not *YOU*
are engaged in drama-based behavior,
taking part in a three-ring circus in the workplace.

You *cannot* control whether or not
other people try to isolate you.

You *can* control whether or not
YOU choose to isolate others.

~ Choice ~

You are the sum of all of your choices to this point: Your choices to move and your choices to be still. You are *who* and *where* you are as a result of your actions and your inactions. And the same goes for everyone you work with. Sure, you've been affected by the actions of others, but your choice in responding to those circumstances is what led you to today. This applies to absolutely everyone. A choice is simply the action that follows a decision. Decision making is what keeps us up at night and running around in circles in the daylight. "What should I do?" is a question you probably ask yourself a dozen or more times a day, and that's just consciously.

Why do people fret over every decision facing them? It's simple. We fear making mistakes. Which, let me tell you, is *such* a waste of time and energy. Our mistakes make us who we are. Bad relationships (including bosses and direct reports) teach us what we DON'T want in the next one, so we ask more questions and choose more carefully next time. Horrible jobs make us thankful for a good one. I'm not recommending that we be foolish in our choices, but making ourselves crazy trying to avoid making a mistake IS a mistake. And not making a decision IS a decision.

I was driving my car the other day around town, returning home from completing some errands and it struck me. All of the people in all of the houses I was passing are going through all sorts of motions to get the work done necessitated by our societal norms. But, do they realize that it's all temporary? That their life could be over later today or tomorrow or in five or ten short years? That no matter how long their life is, it will "soon" be over? So, what does it matter if their lawn is the greenest on the block? Or if they have newly painted siding and a trendy new walkway? And all the people working for companies, pushing paper and having meetings and producing some widget...are they asking themselves "what does it matter?"

This thought bothered me deeply. Super deeply. It's the sort of question that give people insomnia, including me. What's the meaning of all of this "busy-ness" of our "business?" My hypothesis is that being "busy" and caught up in the monotony of the getting through the demands of our daily life keeps us safe from considering that we are all so very temporary on this planet. When we leave this Earth, we will also leave behind a to-do list and countless things that we were on our way to do that will now need to be done by someone else. And, that "someone else" will leave the very same way.

Now, please don't get me wrong. I'm not advocating that you *not* take good care of your lawn, house, job, children, and self. By all means, please do. What I *am* advocating is that you pause to consider what truly brings you joy, gives your life meaning, and makes you feel wholly alive and passionate. Figure out a way to do more of that than anything else. Make THAT the center of your life. Not the lawn. Unless lawn maintenance makes you feel alive and passionate and gives your life meaning. Then have at it! And, please honestly consider expanding your reach and spending some time at my house because my lawn could really use your love.

If you're caught up in a drama at work, ask yourself if "winning" the fight is going to matter on your deathbed? I'm guessing it won't. If you're stressed out 24/7, ask yourself if this was your last day on this planet, is that the mental space you'd want to have held? If you're feeling disconnected and maybe even bullied at work, is that the story that you want as your last experience here? I'm guessing you don't.

In any event, read this loud and clear: You are temporary. Your time on this planet is fleeting. This is powerful news because it means that all the "busy" things you do are far less important than you've been building them up to be. All the dramas and arguments and wrinkles and bruises and bumps are really just inconveniences and distractions from what is <u>really</u> worth your time and energy and love. They don't really matter in the end. If they don't matter in the end, why on Earth do they matter now? Pause on that for a minute. It's a profoundly new way of thinking about things for most people. They don't matter. So, what can you do? Try this exercise.

Exercise: Close your eyes (yes, after you finishing reading this passage, wise guy) and imagine how amazing and successful and joyous those things you are passionate about could be today if you used your energy and your love to build them instead of feeding the dramas, insecurities, stressors, etc. Jot down an estimate of how much time just over the past week that you've spent:

- Doing mundane tasks that really don't build anything of meaning in your life?

- Arguing with or playing out angry or victim-oriented thoughts about other people?

- Circling the emotional or mental drain, beating yourself up about something or other?

- Procrastinating doing what you dream about accomplishing? Starting sentences with "someday...?"

- Pulling other people into the fights you're in and frustrations you're having with other people?

- Being fearful or angry about someone bullying you or shutting you out of things at work?

Remember: Choice got you into the mess you're in, and choice can lead you back out. Maintain a solution-focus. Ask yourself the following questions:

What is standing in the way of me getting the outcome I want?

What can I do to remove those barriers?

Who can I call upon to support me in making a change?

If you focus on the problem, you'll be blind to your choices. If you focus on the possible solutions, you'll empower yourself to take charge and influence the outcome. It's time to take back your power.

We concluded that what you did yesterday (and all those other pesky yesterdays) got you to where you are today, so it follows that if you want to be someplace else in the future, you'll need to start making decisions that are consistent with that future vision of yourself. What *is* your future vision of yourself? Shall we get started with your vision of where and how you'd like to be? Without it you'll just be bouncing between the guardrails of life. First, we have to determine what you have control over and what you don't or you'll be aiming at the wrong targets.

Correct your change agenda by evaluating two things:

1. Are any of your change choices the responsibility of others (a mix-up of your control buckets), and you can only influence them?
2. Are any of the change choices under your control (acknowledging that others influence those things, too)?

If you are in control of your change choice (being more organized, taking better care of yourself physically, etc.), you're still called to examine how others may influence it (a spouse or co-worker messing up your clean workspace, tempting you with bad foods, or disrupting your gym routine). If your change choice is only under your *influence* (a company-wide change), you're called to focus only on your thoughts, feelings, and behaviors in response to the change. When you are aware of where to exercise your power, you can reserve it for where it means something and will make a true difference: First, over the things you can directly control (your thoughts, feelings, and behaviors), and second, over the things you can influence (the thoughts, feelings, and behaviors of others).

Speaking of control, let's explore victims and bullies in the workplace.

"Angry people want you to see how powerful they are. Loving people want you to see how powerful YOU are." ~ Chief Red Eagle

~ Bullying & Control ~

Bullying arises from a misuse of power and a displacement of control. The less intentional bullying occurs often due to an inability to manage stress effectively. There's a culture of intolerance in our society as well as a victim stance from some and victimizing by others. Some people get bullied over and over again and end up, understandably, feeling like a perpetual victim. Bullies see these targets coming from a mile away. For other targets, it's the opposite: Bullies see the target as someone they want to overpower because the target has power that they want for themselves.

One of the inherent problems with taking on a victim stance is that over time, you don't even notice you're doing it anymore. You have now found evidence to support your worldview that you are the victim. If you see someone around you who is doing this, recognize that they probably aren't conscious of it either. Based on circumstances, they are quite sure that they are the victim almost everywhere they go.

~ Forgiveness ~

"Forgiveness does not change the past,
but it does enlarge the future." ~ Paul Boese

There's a useful key to releasing and avoiding the victim stance: Forgiveness. I have a confession: I completely failed. I only dedicated a few paragraphs to this worthy topic in my first book, so now is the time for me to right that wrong and give it the attention it deserves. Why? Because I contend that if we could collectively be better trained in how and when to forgive others we could let go of the baggage that is dragging all of us, our families, or friend circles, our communities, our organizations, and our nations into ugly and destructive places. Holding onto resentments and past wrongs is deadly, literally.

Consider our personal health: It's been well documented that there are serious consequences to holding onto anger. Experiencing anger is normal and utterly human. Living in its grasp is another thing entirely. Letting it take hold of you every day, breathing it in like oxygen, will literally kill you. There are those out there who just don't care, who are blinded by rage and unwavering certainty that they have an impenetrable right to their anger. As I flagged in the beginning of this book, I'm offering a deeply personal example to illustrate a point, to evoke a compassion that will hit this point home.

I sat in a therapy room with my ex-husband many years ago, long after our divorce, and saw this play out in real time. His hatred for me knew no bounds. We sat in that office with one focus: our children. They were suffering, caught in between his rage at me and their love for us both. These little girls just wanted peace and to feel free to love both of us. Instead, they witnessed and experienced his palpable rage at me every day, long after I left him. Anyone who had ever been in a room with the both of us could literally feel his fury.

His eyes burned at me and he would fly into torments without apology or remorse. It was downright toxic to anyone and everyone caught in the crossfire or just bearing witness to it all. Did he have a "right" to be angry? Sure. The reasons for his anger were many and I could psychoanalyze him till the cows come home as to where the rage really emanated from and how "valid" his reasons were.

How much good did that do either one of us, or our children? Absolutely no good. How do I know? Because I tried for years, as did countless therapists, attorneys, judges, friends, and even his own children. In that therapy office that day, the guardian ad litem assigned to our case was trying to convince him that his rage at me was doing catastrophic damage to our children. My ex-husband refused to acknowledge that, citing my actions as the source of his rage, thereby making his rage warranted and unavoidable. The therapist then told him, "the rage that you have in your heart is literally going to kill you. You are going to die from this." My ex-husband's response? If you're hoping an epiphany materialized, thank you, but nothing of the sort occurred. Instead, he said, "I don't care. Then *that woman* will have to explain to my daughters how she caused the death of their loving daddy."

That. That is the blind hatred and conviction that so many people out there in the world embrace on a daily basis and it's killing them. It's poisoning the people around them. It's undermining companies. It's pulverizing profit lines. It is the not-so-silent killer of everything good in the world. Often, it's much more subtle than my ex-husband's so maybe you're not realizing that you're in the midst of it when you are. It often looks like passive-aggressiveness, where you know there's something wrong but no one will directly speak to it. It shows up as blame, where there is no room for shared responsibility over issues, just a villain and a victim. Someone is completely right and someone is irrefutably wrong. That's resentment and contempt and it's poisonous.

What do you do with that? Well, there are three ways you can come across this: as the holder of it, the recipient of it, or as a witness. Whichever role you have in the situation, you're affected. You suffer as a result of it. I'll address tactics you can employ, and share the one thing they share in common: The need to forgive.

If you're the holder of the resentment, you may need a support system to assist you in letting go and getting past these feelings, especially if you've been holding onto them for any period of time. When you feed that demon, you make it much bigger than it started off being, and unraveling it can be very challenging. Having a guide, someone who can validate your experience then move you toward moving through and past it, can be life changing. More than anything, the thing you're going to need to let go of is your need for validation.

Most of us process our anger by talking about it, by getting people to tell us how right we are. When we do that, we reinforce our way of thinking. We calcify our positions and get more and more right about our perspective every time we think or talk about it. We move further and further away from considering how we might be mistaken.

Why does this matter? Simple: We've gotten our egos all tangled up in our resentment, so letting go of the resentment may require that we admit we may have been wrong on some level, that we may have some culpability in the situation. The longer we've maintained our "right" position, the harder it will be to move out of it. The more people we've told about it, the harder it becomes. If we've been bitching about our terrible co-worker for years and created a Batman vs. The Joker scenario, when we do decide to let bygones be bygones, we've got a lot of unpacking to do. If you've been poisoning the well with your anger for some time, you've created factions for and against you and your "enemy." When you decide to get past your feelings, your factions (and theirs) may not follow suit. In an organization, these factions are often solidified by infrastructure built around the conflict. Need an example to illustrate this?

Example:

Andy and Beth have been working at the same company for about three years. Andy works in sales while Beth works in accounting. Their personalities clash with Andy being incredibly direct and loud while Beth is pretty conservative. They butted heads in a meeting not long after they both joined the organization, with each of them making derogatory comments about how each department was handling their aspect of the business.

Over the next few years, their respective departments would mutter with disdain the other person's name (Sales would mock Beth, Accounting would mock Andy). Several instances popped up where Sales was late or inaccurate in requesting things from Accounting, so Accounting retaliated by created complicated policies and procedures aimed at punishing Sales for being "mavericks" and "arrogant." Sales, in turn, handed in projections and reports late to Accounting, refusing to hold themselves accountable to deadlines set by Accounting. Both departments spoke ill of the other in passing and in meetings with other departments.

There were numerous occasions when Andy and Beth (or their counterparts) would fight openly in the halls, in meetings, or loud enough to hear in their offices. The entire organization became affected by their war, being sucked into taking sides as well as just being generally affected by the inefficiencies that their war had implanted in the system. The "us" vs. "them" mindset had become a way of life and everyone was paying the price.

Enter: *Consultant.* I sat Andy and Beth down in a room separately, and engaged each of them in discussions about their conflict: Where it came from, how it got bigger, where it is now? I probed for rationale, and validated their respective positions, knowing that each of them had reasons to be angry and distrusting. I recognized that if they felt like I was not convinced as to why the other person/department was terrible that they'd continue to badmouth the other to get me to side with them. Then, I brought them together. I confirmed with them that the situation had become intolerable and that they knew they needed to change things before upper management came in and removed people to solve the problem their way. I had them write down their complaints on notecards.

Because of the level of conflict, they shared their complaints without speaking about them. After reading the complaints the other person had about them, they wrote down what they pledged to do differently to lessen the conflict by not worsening each complaint. They exchanged cards and let the other person add suggested pledges that would help them to let the past be in the past. They then read their own cards again, and agreed to do these new things, which included going back to their respective departments and getting them on board so the fighting didn't continue department-to-department.

What was key here was *forgiveness*. Forgiveness is the ultimate "f" word. It's touted as being a miraculous cure for emotional unrest. So many memes on social media throw catch phrases around about how useful forgiveness is and how much it benefits the forgiver. How the person can still be a number one putznugget but you're the bigger person so you'll forgive them for their transgressions. It's basically just letting shit go. So why is there such a lack of forgiveness out there? Why is everyone carrying around grudges like teenage girls carry their phones? Because it's just not that simple, and forgiveness flies in the face of everything Americans and materialism and capitalism stand for, or at least so we think.

When I was growing up, forgiveness was a pretty big topic in my household. There was some pretty awful stuff going on, in addition to traumatic historical events, and I was constantly being challenged to forgive. The definition of forgiveness in my house was basically "getting over" whatever had happened. Moving on. Which is all fine and good if: 1) the offense isn't too terrible, and 2) they're not still doing the same thing over and over again. The latter is like being asked to forgive a person for hitting you over the head while they are still hitting you over the head. But that was the requirement in my house. I was quite resistant and I came to the conclusion that I was a bad, unforgiving person. It wasn't until I was in my mid-thirties that I came across a book that forever changed by sense of what forgiveness means and literally transformed my life, personally and professionally.

The book was called "The Shack" (2007) and it described two aspects of forgiveness.

The first aspect was to let go of the hold that the anger and resentment have on you. Having hatred takes a sizeable amount of energy and focus that could be used for other things. It likely gets in the way of forming healthy relationships because your sense of trust and willingness have been lessened. Holding onto that resentment serves to block you from truly taking chances going forward, and poisons you from the inside out. From personal experience, I know I've had a hell of a time letting go of my resentment for others, so let me offer a framework that has made it a much, much easier process. Here's the framework: By holding onto your anger, you are holding onto the event or events that inspired those feelings in you. The person who hurt you has likely moved on and is unaffected.

When you keep this anger at the forefront, you have let go of your power. You have basically handed over your power (your emotions, state of mind, experience of life) to a person that you have negative feelings toward. You are giving them the power to take MORE of your life than you perceive that they already took. Why in the hell would you do that?

Imagine that transaction: Get a visual image of that. Picture yourself holding your joy, smiles, peace, abundance in your hands, placing all of that awesomeness in a basket, and handing it to that person. Seriously? Why would you do that? When I realized that this was what I was doing it hit me HARD. Giving anything more to someone who had hurt me was just downright ridiculous. How dare I do that?

This offers a huge wake-up call. After that, every time I started to get angry or hostile when thinking about them, I paused and imagined handing my basket to them. Thankfully, it was enough to shake me loose from that mental space and move on. Here are a couple of other suggestions for breaking free of the hold that another person's actions have had over you:

Write it allllll down. Yes, write down all their wrongs. Then, do a fearless (and I mean fearless) inventory of what you could have done to lessen, avoid, or prevent the situation (if anything) and how you could have responded differently since that time. This is your contribution to the situation; rest assured, we all have one, no matter how minimal. After you've processed this for a day or two, really taken stock of your role in the situation to the best of your ability, I give you permission to find a safe fire to burn those notes in, repeating something like the following to yourself as their ashes float up into the air: "You no longer have a hold on me. Thank you for the lesson, for the awakening of more strength and understanding." If and when you find yourself reliving any of the ugliness, recant your chosen statement to yourself, reminding yourself, "that's all fine and good, but I've already let that go." It works, people, trust me. It works if you work it...

Write a letter from them to you. Many times, we are angry at and unforgiving toward a person in part because they never said they were sorry. We hold onto our negative feelings, certain that if someday they offer an apology for how they've wronged us that we may then get over it. But that someday never comes. So what then?

Plagarism. Take out some good, old-fashioned paper and pen and write a letter <u>from</u> them <u>to</u> you. It's a letter in <u>their</u> voice, apologizing for what they did and explaining why they did what they did, what part of their humanity led them to behave in that destructive manner. It's what you would hope they would say if they were motivated and aware enough to write it. The pen is in your hand, so write the damn letter.

The second aspect was making a decision about the relationship. Once you've let go of the toxic feelings you've been harboring and freed up the brain space they were renting in your head, it's time to decide if and how you want them in relationship with you.

For some, like co-workers/bosses and certain family members, perhaps you can't make the decision to not have them in your life without severe consequences. You can still decide <u>how</u> you are in relationship with them. You choose how close you want them to be, how much of your time and energy to share, and how deeply you want to trust them. If they've crossed you in the past and you think that they haven't made sufficient changes to avert that behavior in the future, you can choose to hold them at a distance, stiff armed from access to undermining you harshly again. And, because you're smart, you'll know that if they've crossed you before and they haven't changed, they are likely to cross you again.

When they injured you before, you were probably caught by surprise, with the shock itself affecting you on some level. Next time, there won't be any surprises. You'll observe their behavior but not feel shocked or deceived by it. They are simply being themselves. You've established a large enough distance that you aren't leveled by it this time.

Note: If you *are* leveled, this is your call to action, to figure out if there is something you're getting out of the drama of being leveled. Maybe it makes them seem more villainous the more you are suffering? Perhaps you need people to feel badly for you and rally around you?

Those are both quite human, very understandable desires. Own them if you have them instead of hiding behind how another person has done you wrong. People will hurt you. People will be selfish, unthinking, inconsiderate, careless, and downright mean at times. That's a hard fact of life. If you harbor bad feelings each and every time someone behaves badly, that does nothing to change them, as you may have noticed. All it does is poison your own mental pond. It derails *your* success. You're living in a smelly, parasite-infested swamp and wondering why you feel sick.

At the very same time, they are relatively – and perhaps completely – unaffected. Yet you're wasting precious time and energy trying to punish them overtly or in your own mind. That's tantamount to insanity. And, we've all been there. Thinking that if we just get mad enough that something will magically happen; that karma will find them on our behalf. Or, we are convinced that we can make them change and repent by sheer will of thought or the anger we display toward them.

In the words of the infamous Dr. Phil, "how's that working for ya?"

If it has worked for you, please put this book down right this instant and reach out to me. I need to employ a team of scientists and spiritual leaders, and perhaps even Yoda, to understand your fierce mind powers. How DO you do that? Inquiring minds want to know…

For the rest of us, it's time to decide if we'd rather be indignant and "right" or if we'd like to be free and happy. If you imagine a shoulder harness with an enormous amount of weight affixed to it. You're dragging yourself from place to place, struggling to just take a step. Your body aches from the stress of it, and you find yourself getting incredibly irritable and downright furious at the burden you're feeling. You're snappy at people around you, especially those who don't acknowledge what a pain this situation must be for you. You're quick to tell people all about it: "If it wasn't for this harness, everything would be great!" "I can't believe someone put this stupid harness on me. Some people." "It figures. This always happens to me. Someone needs to put a harness on a person and they pick me. Just my luck."

This occurrence is one of the most common in my practice. No matter what department of a company I meet with, the problems they face are another department's fault. In some companies, I have the luxury of working with every department and guess what? They all say that! So, unless there is a mystery creature infiltrating the company and making it look like it's every other department to every other department, chances are the answer is simpler than that. Everyone shares some of the responsibility. Everyone is letting the harness rest on their shoulders. Gloriously, that means that everyone can remove it from their own shoulders.

Example:

I was working with a team of business partners who had been dysfunctional for years before they caught wind of my services and brought me in to assist them. They had established patterns of interacting with one another and they were calcified, assigning motive to one another faster than you could blink. They had built up a boatload of resentments and judgments against one another over the years and their belief that anything could change was lacking.

To complicate matters, they had an outdated and non-applicable business partnership agreement that clearly needed revamping but they couldn't start a conversation about profit-sharing, etc. without it blowing up into a war of the roses. They'd tried tackling it on their own, to no avail. They brought in a contracts expert who also ran into brick walls everywhere he turned.

The issue? Trust.

They wanted proof that the relationship wouldn't head back down that same road. They all wanted to feel respected, understood, and most importantly, *safe*. How do people feel safer, aside from having trust? Taking control. They needed to trust people they didn't currently trust and/or control things they weren't sure how to control (or even influence).

Could I do this for them? Kind of. I'm not them so the heavy lifting clearly couldn't come from me, but I guided them through the process of building trust.

One of the tactics that really helped them was to draft a list of the things they thought would work about their proposed arrangement as well as what might fail. Under each potential failure, they had to offer a pledge of something that they could do to mitigate that downside. They shared those pledges among them to ensure that the hesitations that they had were addressed by the pledges. Each partner needed to hold themselves accountable to their pledges, knowing that without this self-check the entire system would crumble. If they waited for another partner to call them out on coming up short on their pledge, conflict and drama would ensue, pulling them back into old, bad habits.

By owning their own pledges, they built trust in themselves, each other, and hope that the future held something different than the past.

~ Summary ~

You are responsible for getting to this point. If you are angry or resentful toward a person or group or just in general, you have the power to let it go. If you don't, you've let it sap your power. Do you really want to do that? Give your power to people or occurrences that have hurt you? I didn't think so.

Key Chapter Concepts

- Choice and control got you to where you are so they can get you back out.
- Victims and bullies are connected through experience and victims are stuck in victim mode unless they practice forgiveness and reclaim their power.

"Life is an echo. What you send out, comes back.
What you sow, you reap. What you give, you get.
What you see in others exists in you. Remember, life is an echo.
It always gets back to you. So give goodness." ~ Zig Ziglar

ON THE MAIN STAGE

"If you know your enemy and yourself then
every battle is won." ~ Park Tae Seo

~ Path to Engagement ~

If you're going to tame the work circus, you need to
understand the dynamics of *connection* (mixed with a healthy dose of
purpose), otherwise known as *engagement*.

In order to appreciate *connection*, it's key to recognize its
opposite: *isolation.*

It's much like that old adage that hate is not the opposite of
love, apathy is: The lack or presence of love defines the contrast. It's
the same for connection. The lack or presence of connection defines
the contrast: Isolation is the opposite of connection. When you're
fighting, you're still connected, still engaged. When you're isolated,
you're disconnected...unengaged. Engagement is a term that's

bandied about throughout Corporate America as the salve that will cure what ails our business. If people are more engaged, they will work harder, smarter, and bring their companies to the next level of success. Companies coordinate internal "engagement" campaigns, often securing the talents of consultants like yours truly to help them reach higher levels of engagement. They are banking on two main theories about human behavior:

1. People will do more for the things they feel passionate about.
2. People who are happy are more likely to work more effectively and efficiently.

Sounds about right, yes? When you are "into" something you're more likely to dive in and pull out all of the stops to make it happen, right? When you're happy, you're more likely to face each task with a positive, can-do attitude, seeing the roadblocks as less intimidating, correct?

Generally speaking, employees are either focused on achievement or on security. In my terms, they are focused on **purpose** and **validation** or on **control**. Recognizing these motivators helps you to feed their needs as you attempt to engage them and maximize their contributions. When you're trying to get people to feel engaged, it's clearly easier to get the folks with their eyes set on **purpose** to get on board. Are the other folks lost causes? Of course not. They need to know that the purpose of the organization and the connection that you're bringing about will result in them being safe and secure in their jobs. Same result, different pathway. Get it?

We want employees to be engaged one way or the other. The enemy of engagement is isolation. Isolation removes the connection component from engagement which is tantamount to removing peanut butter from a PB&J sandwich and trying to pass it off as a PB&J. Not happening.

To address isolation so that we can reach high levels of engagement, we need to answer a critical question: What does isolation look like in the workplace?

There are three ways to think about isolation:

1. Isolation from the **mission**
2. Isolation from **others** (electronic insulation which can flow from physical separation, remoteness, etc.)
3. Isolation **for power** (as a form of power mongering, aka, bullying)

Three problems, three slightly different interventions required, so let's tackle them separately, shall we?

~ Isolation from the Mission ~

Based on personal experience, if you polled employees (including mid-level executives and a few floundering c-suite executives), you'd find that a vast majority of them haven't a clue as to what their company's mission is. Wait, what? Is that possible? You betcha it is! There are organizations that aren't even sure they *have* one aside from "increasing shareholder wealth" or some such capitalistic priority. Money matters, for sure, but where is the heart in that? Cash is a huge motivator, and for some, it'll do for a while. We've already covered the fact that when people feel purposeful they produce better results, so companies have a payoff to pay attention to what generates those experiences.

Fortunately or unfortunately, human beings need more than money to feel fulfilled, connected, and engaged. When employees don't have a "why" for coming to work every day, putting in all those extra hours, dealing with changes and stressors, and the like, they will burn out. Passion for a mission is like caffeine in the morning: It pumps you up and smacks the life into you to face another challenge.

What's your company's "why?" Why does it exist? How does the work affect people, places, or things? For a mission to be powerful and to evoke passion it needs to stir emotions when you communicate it. It needs to make people pause, reflect, smile, tear up, laugh...something! One of my favorite associations to work with is the Vietnam Veterans of America. Their mission is simple and to call it powerful would be an understatement: "Never again will one generation of veterans abandon another."

For anyone who has ever been connected to a veteran, particularly a Vietnam-era veteran, this statement brings up some pretty strong images and emotions. Just the word "abandon" brings tears to my eyes. Imagine sacrificing your life and then feeling abandoned on the heels of it for the very service you provided? Tragic doesn't begin to cover it. When they start their Board meetings and events they state this mission. It guides everything that they do. They are hell-bent on ensuring that no other veteran ever feels the pain they endured.

Folks, *that* is a mission. That is something you can get behind. I don't care if you make widgets or complete tax returns, you can capture the hearts of your employees – and customers – if your mission is strong, clear, well communicated, and triggers an emotional "why" for getting up every morning and doing business with you.

Grab your coffee 'cause it's activity time!

What is your company's mission? Why does it exist? Who benefits from your services? How do you make life easier for people? How do you support their safety, comfort, joy, connection, passion, etc.? Dig deep, people. This is mission critical (sorry for the pun...I couldn't resist).

The reason my company exists is:

If you've come up with something magnificent, congratulations! If it's still pretty weak and doesn't give you chills when you say it, keep working at it. Enlist some help. Ask a colleague for their thoughts. Get other leadership input. Start a conversation.

Leaders: To bolster the purpose work, create a wish list of what the ideal workplace looks like. Dream it with others. Ask for input at all levels. Be the architect to your perfect workplace vision. What do you want from the culture? If you don't write it down and get buy-in, you can't build it. Be complete. Take your time. Think in terms of what you "don't want" if that helps to spur your thinking.

Trust me when I tell you that doing this work will pay off in spades…times infinity.

~ Isolation from Others ~

In this age of downsizing, reorganizing, cross-functional teams, outsourcing, remote workforces, and international conglomerates, we find ourselves relying more and more on people we've never met in person. We build relationships on conference calls and email threads. We depend on people who are just voices and signature lines to us. It's no small wonder that we:

- Don't feel very connected to one another.

- Aren't as effective getting cooperation and collaboration from others.

- Don't feel a shared mission and priorities.

Physical Insulation as Isolation

How can you develop trust with someone who you are physically disconnected from and you know that you're only getting a part of the picture? If you know that what you see may not be what you get, how does that engender trust? The answer: It doesn't. Without trust, relationships are on shaky ground. People become disposable. It's a whole lot easier to move, demote, layoff, or fire someone you don't have to see face-to-face. This remote workforce, work-from-home, subcontractor environment in modern Corporate America has inserted layers into working relationships that has made them difficult to navigate and has done little to mitigate the negative effects.

Beware of Electronic Insulation:

We say we "know" so-and-so because we've traded emails. Do we really know him? We have what I like to call a mirage of connection….you think it's there, but can you really be sure? What happens when the chips are down? Is that person more likely to help you out or side with the person sitting a cubicle away. Like the folks at Behr paint tell their managers: Focus on getting "belly-to-belly, face-to-face" if you want to build loyalty

We are social beings and we leverage our relationships to get our needs met, personally and professionally. When we aren't in close contact and shared space with the people who help us to get our jobs done, we lose much of that leverage. The phrase "having to face someone" when we've harmed them (by omission or commission) doesn't apply to a large proportion of our work relationships. We can hide behind an email response that we've missed a deadline or are shifting a project. We don't have to look in someone's eyes to share the bad news. We don't have to be courageous; we get to hide. We hide behind the veil of electronic communication so we are insulated from the effects of our actions (or inactions).

For those of us who grew up in neighborhoods where kickballs were likely to end up in Mrs. Murphy's yard (or, worse, through her window), our parents taught us to own up to our mistakes by knocking on her door and fessing up, offering to replant the smashed flowers or doing chores to pay to fix the window. We now live in a duck-and-cover society where we play the blame game so the injured party is often uncertain as to who did what. We have legions of lawyers deployed to fight our battles and cover up our mistakes.

Despite what the slogans on the wall in the office say, we avoid accountability, and in doing so we infect ourselves with an organizational cancer.

How so? When you're not accountable (and when those around you aren't), you're more likely to behave badly because the consequences don't directly follow the action. When people are behaving badly and getting away with it, trust erodes. People don't feel like they can count on one another which creates tension which leads to conflict, turning to stress and often coming out as drama. It's a beautifully disturbing thread through an organization that demands our immediate attention and intervention.

Keyboard Courage

You've probably heard the term "beer muscles," referring to the bravado that often accompanies imbibing of alcohol. The office has its own version of this: "keyboard courage." This term refers to the phenomenon whereby people develop the courage to say things via text and on email that you'd never say face-to-face. Very few of us would fly off the handle face-to-face but countless legions of us will say snarky, passive aggressive, and downright aggressive and insulting things to people over email. We pride ourselves in the zingers we deliver, putting someone else (who is somehow deserving of this treatment because they "had it coming") in their "place." If we'd seen the recipient in person, we were likely to be a bit gentler, collaborative, and compromising. The social isolation we have constructed in our workforce therefore supports practices that serve to further disconnect people.

How can we mitigate this damage?

Praise in public, criticize in private. If you have something negative to say to someone or about the status of a project, pick up the phone and speak to them. Make sure that there are no missing pieces or misunderstanding. Selfishly, this affords you the chance to correct any errors on your end that might be hanging out there, waiting for someone to pounce on. It protects egos but not airing the dirty laundry out in public. Most importantly, it puts the interests of the company above any one or more individuals. The company benefits from some pretty simple things: happy employees, happy customers, good products, and strong profits. None of those things are improved when employees are at each other's throats or throwing each other under the bus. They are *all* improved when employees are experiencing lower levels of conflict, more supportive relationships with their colleagues, and processes that aren't thwarted by workplace drama.

~ Isolation for Power ~

This kind of isolation is the ugliest form of all. This isolation is intentional because isolating an individual or group is done in order to minimize the target's influence, credibility, effectiveness, or to downright punish them. It can be *physical*, as in sending a certain department to the furthest, darkest reaches of the building. It can be *interpersonal*, as in luring people to side against you by discrediting, maligning, and embarrassing you. It's ostracism. It's a form of bullying, or the taking of power and influence by force. When people are isolated by a bully, they often lose credibility and influence over their responsibilities because their effectiveness is undermined by the interference of the bully. The effects of this on companies are catastrophic.

A study out of Canada (O'Reilly, Berdahl, & Banki, 2014) revealed that:

> People who claimed to have experienced ostracism were significantly more likely to report a degraded sense of workplace belonging and commitment, a stronger intention to quit their job, and a larger proportion of health problems.

Smart companies are taking this issue head on. Google has a "no jerk" policy that is implemented at the interview stage in an attempt to prevent the jerks from even coming in for orientation. Jerk behavior often leads to ostracism of one or more targeted employees. Sometimes, people ostracize their co-workers because they don't know how else to handle the conflict so ignoring and shutting them out seems reasonable. Plus, it's a passive approach so it's less likely that the person doing it will be held accountable like they might if they openly confronted or harassed the person. Heading these (overt and covert) behaviors off at the pass is always a smart approach. If not, there must be a zero-tolerance policy. If it's tolerated, it becomes a fast-spreading cancer that will be more difficult (and expensive) to eradicate.

"The more I want to get something done,
the less I call it work." ~ Richard Bach

~ Securing Engagement ~

We've discussed previously that:

Stress is the brought on by experiencing the difference between what you *seek to control* and what you *actually can control.*

That's what causes stress in the workplace: Seeing an issue and not having the perceived power to influence its solution. This is a call to employers to do three key things:

1. Empower their employees to have a say in fixing things
2. Teach the key lessons in this chapter about what you can control vs. what you can influence
3. How to increase your influence through attitude, role modeling, and relationships

When you put people in control of things, you increase their investment in the work and the outcome. They are vested. Vested is just another word for engaged which pays off in spades for companies. When people are engaged, they are valuing the outcome for the company above other factors. They want the best for the company. They are connected to the mission, the work, and the organization. The same works in reverse. If they are lacking engagement, your company will feel it throughout, even in the bottom line.

What can you do to promote engagement within your organization? I've described below some pretty straightforward interventions and approaches to funnel the power that an engaged workforce offers.

Focus on connection: Especially in times of change, people need more connection. Get to know your people. Make sure that they know that they matter to you, to the division, to the company. When in doubt, reach out. It's really as simple as that. I can't tell you how many times an executive has shared a dilemma they are facing at work and when I ask, "did you speak to them about it?" their answer is, "no." C'mon people: The shortest distance between two points is a straight line. Walk it for crying out loud. Bring people together whenever possible. Speak with people by phone or in person as much as possible, particularly when there's an issue. Resist putting conflicts into email without talking first.

Focus on mission: Share it openly and often. Start every all-hands meeting by stating it out loud. Lead other managers to challenge people to consider it in their daily dealings by asking questions like, "how does this decision communicate our mission?" Integrate it in everything you do and you will attract and retain people who want to see it come alive.

Focus on passions: This comes down to knowing your people and what makes them tick. If you know what they are confident doing and what they enjoy doing (hopefully the same thing), see if you can have them do more of that. When your passions are fueled, just like your "high" feeling after exercise, you are invigorated and almost hungry to tackle the next challenge. Imagine the power of that for an organization…harnessing that would be life – and company – changing.

Focus on recognition: People feel most connected to the things they are confident about being good at. Tell them they are doing well when they are doing well. Provide incentives for them to do better. Make sure the incentives resonate with their motivation system. The more flexible, the better. Think of your mileage program: You can take your rewards in a number of ways: Save up for a big trip, get cash back, receive gift cards….when you give choice in recognition you empower people to own the reward in a way that they are certain to appreciate it.

Focus on forgiveness: I've found that most employees start their jobs, like any relationship, full of hope and excitement. They left another lackluster position for this one because it promised something special. Somewhere along the way, the shine wore off and they started pulling away from their excitement for their current job.

When that happens, engagement falls off. If, in the process, they've become known for not being a strong contributor, see that through the lens of them not feeling engaged versus being a poor employee. Forgive their (natural) response to the lack of engagement. Press the "reset" button. See if you can stir up that initial excitement and engage them and their talents again. It's sometimes easier (and usually cheaper) to rehabilitate a current employee than to find and engage a new one.

> "At the end of the day, it's not what you have
> or even what you've accomplished.
> It's about who you've lifted up,
> who you've made better.
> It's about what you've given back." ~ Denzel Washington

~ Connection Conundrum ~

We are more connected, yet less connected, than ever before.

We are constantly connected to our devices. Raise of hands: Where is your phone? Within arms' reach. Where is your phone when you sleep? Within arms' reach. Who has their phone in the BATHROOM with them? Most. We post, we tag, we like, we share, we blog, we follow. Do we CONNECT? We connect behind the glass. Behind pretense. Behind barriers that filter out what we don't want to share or risk. Electronic communication has made it so that you can edit your thoughts before you share them. They are open for wild misinterpretation, but they are sanitized nonetheless.

What do I mean by sanitized? When you're texting or emailing someone, you can hit the backspace bar as many times as you want before you hit "send." Okay, sometimes autocorrect can thwart you, but you can be in control of what you say right down to the chosen emoticon. In person? Not so much. It's real time. If you say the wrong thing, it's out there in the Universe and you're accountable. Electronic communication removes that risk. It's why people are more inclined to say audacious and threatening things electronically that they'd never say in person. It's electronic insulation. And a powerful phenomenon. It insulates us from risk, yet it opens us up to great risk. We can be brave and say something, anything, and then we hit "send" and it's out there, permanently. You can try to explain it or frame it later, but it's out there, forever. You can't say, or even think, that you didn't say a certain thing. There it is, in black and white.

People take risks electronically which can mimic certainty or confidence and can feel like connection. I suppose it is at some level, but it's not necessarily replicated when you are in person with one another. Seeing someone's name pop up in your inbox over a series of months and trading emails back and forth can make it seem as though you're "connected," but are you really? Isn't that what life is all about? Connecting with other people? Sharing life's ups and downs, side by side? Being face-to-face and considering in the moment and ahead of time what might be the right or wrong thing to do or say? Being real. Vulnerable. In the moment.

That's really what we've _lost_ and _gained_ in our tech-dependent world: _Control._ Control in our connections.

We want to control how we are perceived and accepted. Yet, if we were honest and clear we would recognize that we can only contribute to the perceptions others have of us; we cannot control them. They have their own mental frameworks and agendas and baggage and our actions filter through all of that. We've all seen examples of people who seemed to "have it all" but when you peek behind the curtain what you see is a chaotic mess of a life, fraught with more challenge, sadness, and unrest than anything you're dealing with. There are so many among us who expend a great deal of energy crafting a façade to fool others (and often, themselves) into thinking that their life is grand and the path they are on is right and steady. The reality couldn't be further from the truth. This disconnect makes relationships of any kind, professional or personal, incredibly difficult to navigate. What you see may or may not be what you get. When that is the reality, trust is low. Speaking of relationships…

~ Relationship Contracts ~

"Expectation is the root of all heartache." ~ William Shakespeare

Did you know that you have a relationship contract with everyone in your life? You don't remember signing it? You did. You agreed to a set of expectations that each of you could have about each other. Expectations that may or may not have been discussed, but that each of you hold about the other person. Maybe it's that they will always tell you the truth, no matter how potentially hurtful. Maybe it's that you will always keep things light and cheerful, staying away from anything deep and meaningful. People sign these contracts every day when they enter into relationships and set up their "dance," their relationship dynamic. Figuring out what those contracts are is worth investigating. Why?

Ahh, so many reasons. First off, I'm a huge proponent of awareness. If you are aware of something, you can make deliberate actions versus just going along for the ride. Second, when you see your relationships as based on these contracts, you can see how certain agreements might not be serving you. You can appreciate that it's not necessarily about who the other person is or who you are; it's about the relationship contract you both signed. Lastly, when you can see your relationship contracts clearly, you can trust the people you're in relationship with to be exactly as the contract spells out. Well, that is, unless or until they decide to change the contract.

Contract Shifts

In the beginning of my coaching career I had an executive coaching client who met me at a professional workshop and was intrigued by my unique approach. Grayson was a C-level executive who struggled personally and interpersonally in his leadership roles. He had a short temper and tended to dramatize everything. When I spoke with him it was somewhat like chatting with my girlfriends in high school. Many phone calls were kicked off with "you're not going to believe THIS." Our coaching focus was on centering, calming, and strengthening him to deal with his inner demons that were hell-bent on undermining him at every turn. His insecurities approached paranoia at times. No matter how much success he was enjoying, he was always waiting for the other shoe to drop, to fail somehow.

I coached him on and off for years. He would tidy himself up after a bit, then call me again when he'd fallen down again and I'd swoop into help him pick himself back up. During one of our periods of work together, I met with his executive team to do some work to advance his agenda with his new organization. He was not present during our meeting, as was planned in advance so that I could get them to speak freely. Since he was out of town during the meeting, he reached out to me after I left the worksite to get a debrief on the meeting. I had only a minute to spend with him before my plane took off so I tried to be succinct. I reported all good things, especially that I was making headway in shifting their mindsets about change and responsibility. Just as I had to shut my phone down I told him that we would catch up later about the rest of the meeting. This piqued his interest. He pressed but I told him I'd rather cover it all in detail when I had more time (the flight attendant was hovering over me, telling me to shut down my phone). He pressed more so I said, "the staff shared some thoughts and needs they have relative to their relationship with you." I then told him one last time that I had to shut down the phone and I'd check in when I landed.

While I was in flight, he peppered me with incredibly long, emotional, critical, and accusatory texts. He had almost three hours to stew in his own juices as to what these "thoughts and needs" were and he railed at me. He accused me of being disloyal. Of undermining him. Of ganging up on him with his staff. Amidst all of these texts over those few hours, he terminated my work with him and his company. Fired me. I couldn't respond until an hour after his diatribe had settled in and by then his anger and position had calcified. He was certain that I had failed him and that it was beyond the point of no return.

If you think for a minute that I let it go and walked away, you need to get to know me a bit better. I'm like a pitbull on a porkchop and I was not going quietly into the night. I also knew that fighting him and telling him how wrong he was for making all of these assumptions, particularly because he didn't even know what was said in that meeting, was not going to get me to my desired outcome. What was my desired outcome? The two things I wanted were to:

1. **Clarify:** For him to know the truth (so I could at least be judged and evaluated on what really happened, not on what he imagined to have happened).

2. **Salvage:** To preserve the relationship and therefore the job (as much joy as my job brings to me, I do have a family to support).

How did I proceed, trying to clarify and salvage? I followed my own advice, that's what I did. I texted him and asked if we could speak by phone, just to close things out. How did that help? I wasn't fighting him and trying to "win" him over. I was accepting his position without question. When I called, I started by meeting him where he was, telling him that I completely understood how angry he would be given his assumptions about what had happened. I then let him know that it might be helpful for him to know what happened so that he would be best prepared for working with his staff going forward. Once I shared what happened, he softened. He held his ground – being angry – for a while (our conversation lasted almost two hours). I just listened and clarified what actually happened so he could hear that he wasn't being undermined or threatened or deceived by anyone, including me. By the end of the phone call, he had eased up, backed off of my termination, and thanked me for my time and support.

No, it wasn't a Jedi mind trick. Well, maybe it was, but I'll bet that it can work for you, too. Focusing on the *intention* for the relationship (to preserve it and have it be based on truth) and *validating* his experience were the only tricks in my bag. The situation offered a hot bed of stress, drama, and impending isolation if I let myself be lured into his overreaction. What did I already know about him? That he thrived on drama and stress; that overreaction was his mainstay. If I participated in that I was sure to make things worse. You can't wrestle a pig in mud and expect to win. They like the mud and they're better at it.

What on earth does this have to do with relationship contracts? Absolutely everything. Relationship contracts are all about expectations and trust. Relationships of all kinds (personal and professional) go off the rails when people expect people to be different than they are or when people attempt to change the relationship contract after they've entered into it. When either of these things happen, stress, drama, and/or isolation follow.

I knew who Grayson was pretty soon after we started our work together. I knew that he was likely to feel paranoid if he thought that I had done anything to compromise his leadership position or respect. I also knew that once he went to that paranoid place, trying to talk him out of it straight on was going to be quite ineffective and would only serve to harden his position. Think about it: When you feel like someone is out to get you, are you likely to believe them when they tell you that they're not? Nope. Our relationship contract looked a little like this:

> "Grayson gets to feel crazy and overwhelmed and paranoid and Bridget's job is to calm, center, and strengthen him. Bridget needs to tolerate whatever Grayson throws at her, knowing that this is why they are working together: To make him a better leader by being a better person first."

My client didn't violate the contract we had. He kept it. I didn't violate it, either, but I did put it to the test by opening the door that invited his insecurities to take hold in our work together, to question my loyalty to him. The lesson I learned has stayed with me in the years since this encounter: When the relationship shifts (as it did when we expanded my reach into his team), the relationship contract needs to be revisited. If that isn't done consciously and directly, stress, drama, and/or isolation are sure to follow.

This is your cue to assess your relationship contracts, to see if they serve you and/or if they need to be assessed. Here are some questions to ask yourself about your relationships (personal or professional) to see if your contracts might need to be updated or rewritten entirely.

- What are the rules about your relationship (who is allowed/supposed to do what?)?

- What have you agreed to that now feels uncomfortable or bad?

- Are there déjà vu moments where you're aggravated again about something that went on between you?

See anything interesting? Think it might be time to renegotiate?

Before I came to understand relationship contracts, I had a huge issue with trust. I expected people to act like I would act, which was good in some cases and not so much in others. I'm not perfect (shocking, I know) so I would sometimes imagine that people would behave like "bad" me which was scary. Like you, I'd been hurt in the past and vowed to never let it happen it again. But it did, over and over again. I trusted less and less as time went on. I was left feeling anxious and resentful. When I was able to see the contracts in my relationships, the ways in which I agreed to be a certain way and tolerate a certain level of behavior from others, I began trusting people to be who they are, where they are. A magical thing happened that changed my life forever: My expectations about others started to equal reality. Expectations equaled reality. I wasn't falling from the tower of expectations onto the cold, hard ground of reality. They were one in the same.

This process is not about lowering your expectations; it's about *righting* them. You can trust absolutely everyone: To be who they are, in the situation they are in, conditions they are under, and within the contract they signed. Putting *our* hopes and expectations on others instead of simply observing them gets in the way of our happiness and initiates all kinds of stress.

Please don't get me wrong: I have screwed this up plenty of times since. I have this pesky little thing called "hope" that gets in the way of having expectations equal reality. I *hope* that people will be who I need them to be instead of who they are. I let my hope for my needs getting met (someday) to eclipse what they are likely to do. What's that saying? "Inspect before you expect." You can better align expectations with reality when you're informed.

Character is demonstrated by actions, not words. Watch what people do; what they spend their time and money on. It's very revealing. When someone tells you that you are important to them and that they value things about you that their other relationships don't offer, but then they opt to spend their time and resources on those other relationships, believe their actions. It might sound nicer in their head to say that they value the things they say they do, but the truth is revealed in their actions. Who you are is who you spend the most time with and invest the most energy in. Be careful. As Maya Angelou said,

"People show you who they are. Believe them the first time."

Here's a visual to keep in mind the next time you're tempted to expect someone to be someone who you want them to be versus who they've shown themselves to be:

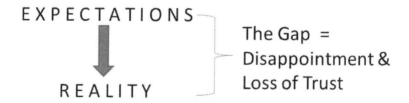

Property of Dr. Bridget Cooper, 2015

The fall from expectation to reality hurts. We call it "disappointment." How much does it hurt when someone calls you a "disappointment?" Or tells you that you've disappointed them? It's hard to hear. We've fallen from grace. How do we get ourselves tangled up in these disappointments over and over again? It goes back to trust and understanding. When I say "trust" I mean choosing how much you should trust. When I say "understanding" I don't mean blind compassion and being a doormat. I meant that you really have to:

Trust people to be who they are, where they are.

If you trust your co-worker to have your back when your co-worker is on a performance improvement plan and is at risk of losing his job, then you're going to be disappointed. Even if you're friends, I advise you to see things from their perspective. What needs do they have that are being shortchanged? If they are being counseled for their poor performance, chances are they aren't getting their need for **control** (being able to create the outcome of the performance improvement plan) and **validation** (being offered positive feedback) fed, and perhaps also their need for **purpose** (excitement about their job) and **connection** (positive relationship with their supervisor and perhaps their co-workers).

If you trust your friend/co-worker to be chummy with you in the workplace when focused on trying to keep her job, you're going to feel let down. Did she not used to act like a friend? She's different now because her priorities are different there based on her choices and desires: To survive professionally. She might jump in front of a moving train for you when you're socializing in the city on the weekend. But if she's desperate to keep her job, make no mistake: She might be just this side of cordial at the office if she perceives that anything beyond that may be seen as unprofessional.

This gap answers the question: What is the difference between *expectations* and *reality* of any given situation, person, and experience? Are your expectations far from the reality of the situation, person, or yourself? Are you constantly disappointed? Or, does it depend on the person or circumstance? Do you have magical thinking or are you grounded in harsh reality? Can you easily accept what is real versus what you want or do you usually confuse hope with good sense? Do you trust people or situations before fact-checking? Reducing the difference between what you're expecting from yourself, others, and situations and what you are likely to experience will make you far more effective, calm, and successful.

As you can see, these gaps can run the gamut. What matters is how you use your characteristics, if your results are positive, how close your expectations are to reality, and that you observe and attend to these gaps with a high level of consciousness and proactivity. The gap between where you are and where you want to be is simply a series of steps and corrections. When you identify the source of your pain you can work to ease it.

~ Summary ~

Tapping into the power of engagement is a formidable, but worthwhile challenge. As with anything, attending to the factors that support it as well as those that threaten it bring you closer to the finish line. Understanding the types of isolation can help you to avoid, mitigate, or change them. Recognizing how expectations that are out of whack with realty can derail connection empowers you to take charge of your connections. Put together, you can dominate this thing we call engagement.

> **Key Chapter Concepts**
>
> - Engagement is the blend of connection and purpose.
> - The opposite (and enemy) of engagement is isolation.
> - Consider how close your expectations are to reality.
> - There are three types of isolation: Isolation from mission, isolation from people, and isolation for power.

"Every terrorist regime in the world uses isolation to break people's spirits." ~ *Bell Hooks*

10

FOLDING UP THE BIG TOP

"There are far, far better things ahead
than any we leave behind." ~ C.S. Lewis

~ It's Beaver Time ~

I know, I know. I've written a book about the work circus and I'm now making beaver references? What kind of crazy logic is that? It's my logic. It's my book and I get to do what I want. Who's to say that beavers don't belong in the circus anyway? Oh, that's right, they *don't!* The whole point of this book is to use your leadership acumen and personal accountability to tame the circus at work, to remove yourself from the main show and sideshow acts and forge a new pathway. It's all about NOT being a circus animal. Opting out of the drama and the stress and the isolation.

Enter: The beavers.

A friend of mine wrote about beavers...how they use the natural resources in their environment to make a home for themselves. They use their strong, sharp teeth to cut down trees, working together, of course. I don't know that any one beaver has ever made a go of it and lived solo, so teamwork is a factor in Beaverville, as well. How do they build these homes? They use the trees to build dams so they can live peacefully and protected together in still water. Where water is flowing, they put a stop to that! What's the lesson I'm imparting here? It's simple:

Be a beaver!

A number of you out there are chuckling right now, but that will make this lesson that much easier to remember now won't it?

Be a beaver. If you see a problem and you need a solution, do what is necessary to make that happen. Work together whenever possible. Keep it simple. Focus on the outcome. Watch for predators. Have each other's backs. Plan ahead. If the tree is about to fall but it's slow going, stay with it. Call in reinforcements. Don't start over at another tree when you've invested all that effort in the first one.

~ To My Female Colleagues Out There ~

We must remember to be graceful in our relationships with one another. Men are less a threat to our sanctity and success than women are, unfortunately. We eat our own. We must stop that. We must realize that we are not in competition with one another for scarce resources. Resources are truly abundant, endless actually, if we pay attention. We can share the stage, and build more stages.

~ To You, My Fierce Reader ~

To all you people out there who think that being strong, centered, and downright badass means that you are never played for the fool, taken advantage of, or feel weak and crushed: No way, no how. There are a multitude of fierce, capable executives out there who have been on the short end of a thorn-covered stick, including me. Our good nature has been pirated for someone else's benefit, sometimes many times over, unfortunately. It's not whether or not you get knocked down or fall on your own sword: It's how you pick yourself up off of the floor, brush yourself off, tend to your wounds, and move the hell forward. It's how you take the ass whippings that life gives you and turn them into what makes you a positive, contributing warrior of life and work.

My work here is done, yet yours has just begun. I'm not abandoning you, though. My words and guideposts are here, in this book. And, if you need me – and there's no shame in needing assistance – I'm out here, now that I've been paroled from book writing. I'm here to help you take back your personal power so that you can put more of your natural goodness, aptitude, and persona into the world. The world needs you. We only have a short stint here and we'd best use it for good, for growth, for prosperity (on so many fronts). It's cliché but it fits: Life isn't a dress rehearsal.

Ready for the main stage in your own life versus the circus you've been recruited to? Your cage rattler awaits you…

Peace,

Dr. B.

bridget@drbridgetcooper.com

"Anything that annoys you is teaching you patience.
Anyone who abandons you is teaching you how to stand up on your own two feet.
Anything that angers you is teaching you forgiveness and compassion.
Anything that has power over you is teaching you how to take your power back.
Anything you hate is teaching you unconditional love.
Anything you fear is teaching you courage to overcome your fear.
Anything you can't control is teaching you how to let go." ~ *Jackson Kiddard*

#

QUICK REFERENCE SECTION

"I like things to happen. And if they don't happen,
I like to make them happen." ~ Winston Churchill

I'm providing this chapter for your ease in referencing back to some of the tidbits in this book that you might not immediately know where to find. You're welcome. ☺

~ Premise of the Book & Taking Back Your Power ~

The way you think about things creates…

The way you feel about things which creates…

The way you act upon things.

This, in turn, creates your experience.

~ The Four Core Needs ~

Control: People like to be in control, often of circumstances, events, and other people. The world is a scary place on a host of levels and the more control we are able to have, the less fearful we become. Phrases like, "you got this" and "master of his domain" come from this assertion. When you're "large and in charge" you're touting the fact that you're in control. It feels good to be in control because the opposite is to be out of control and no one likes that.

Connection: We are social beings. We crave connection with others to varying degrees. We want to be in relationships with others to our level of comfort (think, extrovert vs. introvert). Sometimes we connect in unhealthy ways just to serve the need to be connected.

Purpose: The pinnacle dilemma most people face over the course of their lives is answering the question: "Why am I here?" It's the traditional mid-life crisis conundrum. For employees, it's about having a reason for getting up every day, putting on your suit, and braving the stressors that work brings.

Validation: We like to feel like we matter, like we are valued, like we are appreciated. At work, so many people feel overlooked for their contributions and investments in the company, often only getting feedback from their leaders when things are going wrong (or at annual review time).

~ The Triple Threat to Organizational Culture ~

Stress: The growing and ever-present phenomenon of feeling incapable of getting done what needs to get done or perform or feel the way you want to feel.

Drama: The exaggeration of normal human interactions that makes small problems bigger than they need to be by involving emotion, additional players, and widespread attention.

Isolation: Has a physical and an interpersonal component. *Physical isolation* refers to the distance that people physically have from one another. *Interpersonal isolation* is the lack of belonging or connectedness you feel with your colleagues.

~ Triple Threat Pathways ~

Stress leads to Drama	When you're stretched thin you are apt to react emotionally.
Stress leads to Isolation	Sometimes you shut people out when you're overloaded, choosing a task- vs. a people-focus.
Drama leads to Isolation	When someone is overly emotional they can get tossed from informal networks and be undermined by others.
Drama leads to Stress	Does this really need an explanation?
Isolation leads to Stress	Whether it's from bullying or another source, people need connections for social reasons and to get things done. When they can't, it gets stressful.
Isolation leads to Drama	When people are isolated, they are apt to act out to get their needs met.

**Stress is the pressure felt when what you *want to control*
is greater than *what you can actually control.***

~ Stop, Center, Move Approach to Focus & Power ~

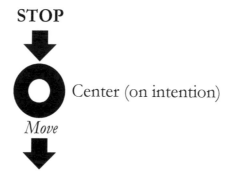

Property of Dr. Bridget Cooper, 2015

Stop what you're doing, thinking, saying. **Center** on what you want out of the next interaction. **Move** toward your intention.

~ Fear-Trust-Control Model ~

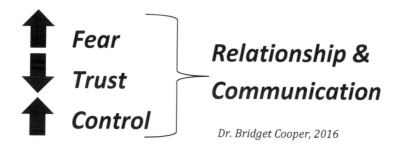

Dr. Bridget Cooper, 2016

~ Agility Matrix ~

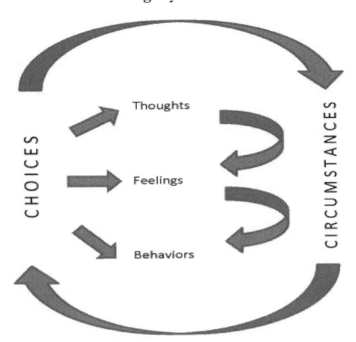

Property of Dr. Bridget Cooper, 2015

~ The Three Hallmarks of Emotional Agility ~

4. **Insight** – Understanding people and oneself, seeing motivations, aware of stuff beyond the "chatter" or "noise" of what the problem may look like on the outside.

5. **Distance-ability** – Decreasing emotional and reactive response by being able to create distance and perspective about the situation.

6. **Flexibility** – Thinking and behaving differently in response to internal and external cues.

~ Power of Acceptance Model ~

Acceptance ⬌ Peace ⬌ Power/Influence

~ Control Conundrum Meets the Triple Threat ~

You *cannot* control whether or not *other people* are stressed out.

You *can* control whether or not YOU are stressed out.

You *cannot* control whether or not *other people*
are engaged in drama-based behavior,
creating a three-ring circus in the workplace.

You *can* control whether or not YOU
are engaged in drama-based behavior,
taking part in a three-ring circus in the workplace.

You *cannot* control whether or not *other people* try to isolate you.

You *can* control whether or not YOU choose to isolate others.

~ Three Types of Isolation ~

1. Isolation from the **mission**

2. Isolation from **others** (electronic insulation which can flow from physical separation, remoteness, etc.)

3. Isolation **for power** (as a form of power mongering, aka, bullying)

~ Expectations vs. Reality ~

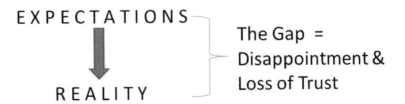

Property of Dr. Bridget Cooper, 2015

*"Character cannot be developed in ease and quiet.
Only through experience of trial and suffering can the soul be strengthened,
ambition inspired, and success achieved. ~ Helen Keller*

ABOUT THE CAGE RATTLER

"There is only one way to avoid criticism:
do nothing, say nothing, and be nothing." ~ Aristotle

Dr. Bridget Cooper has been rattling cages since she was knee high to a grasshopper it seems. For companies and individuals she continues that work, helping them to see the ways they imprison themselves away from the full potential of their work and their lives. She is a Change Strategist. Thought Shifter. *She guides people to be better leaders by being better people first.* Her drive is to help people to be clear, passionate, and invigorated about their lives and work so that they will propel their organizations toward success, establish stronger teams, healthy work climates, positive working relationships, and happier clients and customers. Her forte is leading high-level cultural change initiatives, particularly those with longstanding conflict. She also develops and delivers custom-designed, interactive, and motivational organizational development interventions taking the form of executive strategic planning retreats and conflict interventions as well as training seminars on: effective communication, conflict resolution, relationship building, productivity, finding your passion and purpose, time management, and decision making and problem solving.

Through her education and experience, she understands relationship dynamics and approaches her work from a systemic and holistic perspective. She consults on leadership and entrepreneurial challenges for a variety of companies, and is practiced and available as a keynote speaker on any range of leadership and service topics. She has conducted seminars, retreats, delivered keynotes, and led change initiatives for numerous associations and organizations including: United Technologies Corporation, L-3 Communications, Girl Scouts of Connecticut, Vietnam Veterans of America, Computershare, WirelessZone, Gateway Financial Partners, The Phoenix, Junior League of Washington, Department of Defense, Allied World Assurance Company, Believe, Inspire, Grow (B.I.G.) Connecticut, Connecticut Society of Association Executives, Glastonbury Chamber of Commerce, Connecticut Boards of Education, American Massage Therapists Association, CT Apartments Association, Metacon Gun Club, Women's Independence Network (WIN), Connecticut Associated Builders & Contractors, L-3 Communications, Hartford Dental Society, Bethany College, Draeger Medical Systems, The George Washington University, USA Weekend, Women In Business Summit, TANGO, and American Case Management Association. She ran a monthly empowerment workshop for women ("First Wednesdays") in addition to local presentations for Believe, Inspire, Grow (B.I.G.) of Connecticut for women entrepreneurs. She was selected as a special guest "Game Changers Day 2015" at Lauralton Hall and has been the featured closing keynote speaker for the Greater Hartford Women's Conference two years running.

Raised in New England, she earned her B.S. with a concentration in human resource management from the University of Massachusetts, her M.A. in marriage and family therapy at the University of Connecticut, and her Ed.D. through the educational leadership program at the George Washington University. Her dissertation was on the social network structures of women in academic medicine.

Dr. Cooper has been a leader in the Girl Scout organization, President of the Parent-Teacher Organization, soccer coach, religious education instructor, and elementary school room parent and activity chairperson. Prior to her move to Connecticut, she served as an instructor in conflict resolution and anger management for inmates of the Fairfax County Adult Detention Center. Her hobbies include traveling to places far and wide and seeking out photo opportunities of people, places, and things. She has a never-ending bucket list that she's slowly checking off, and she takes suggestions.

She has three other books aimed at assisting organizations and individuals solve their personal and interpersonal challenges. Her last book, "Stuck U.," guides readers through her five-step change process at the individual and organizational level, shedding light on the core competencies that make or break change initiatives. "Feed The Need" (2014), will change the way you think about problems, and strengthen and empower you to solve them. In this groundbreaking book, you will discover how to identify, understand, and feed your core emotional needs so that you can live more harmoniously with yourself and others and resolve any conflict more effectively. She adapted this guide for teenagers in "Feed The Need: Teen Edition" (2014), with a foreword written by an inspiring high school student.

Please contact her to gain her insight and partnership on solving your personal, professional and organizational challenges at bridget@drbridgetcooper.com or by visiting her website at www.drbridgetcooper.com.

Testimonials about Dr. Cooper's
Thought Shifting, Cage Rattling, Change Strategy

"Dr. Cooper masterfully crafted a well-written and easy-to-understand self-assessment tool [**Power Play**] that magically doubles as a simple to follow escape map leading to the warm and loving light of a happier, healthier and more fulfilling workplace existence." *Private Equity Investor & Serial Entrepreneur*

"I've been attending and running leadership retreats for many years and Bridget is by far the most effective facilitator I've ever experienced." *Board Member, Connecticut Society of Association Executives*

"I will be recommending you to everyone I speak to. This was the best Board retreat I've ever been to, and I've been to a lot over the years." *Board Member, Glastonbury Chamber of Commerce*

"With Bridget on my team, I now have a Coach that leads me to be a leader. I had ideas when we began, I now create ideas. I had goals when we began, I now achieve. I had thoughts when we began, I now dream. And what's most awesome: I am led to live my dream." ~ *Executive Coaching Client, Colorado*

"Bridget is one of those people that carries a sense of calm with her no matter the audience she faces. As a person, she is intuitive, a phenomenal listener, and a positive spirit. As a consultant, she is a critical thinker that captures the essence of what is happening in real time in order to translate it in a meaningful way for all participants." *Associate Director, TANGO*

"I have had the great fortune to work with Bridget on a few different occasions and am better off as a result. She has a unique and distinct knack for very quickly becoming a member of the team(s) she is working with, giving her a great deal of trust and camaraderie with the group. Without fail, she stays focused on result, even if it means changing course during our sessions. Her goal isn't just to follow a script, sadly an experience I have had in some cases, but rather to involve herself in the team and work to result. I'm confident when I learn that Bridget is facilitating any meetings that they will be quite successful! Bridget's personality, in my opinion, is another factor that will continue to set her apart. As mentioned earlier, she gets acquainted with those she is working with, allowing her to blend at a somewhat personal level while maintaining very high standards of professionalism and integrity." *VP of Information Technology, Draeger*

"You changed, and saved, my life." *Executive Coaching Client*

"You know our audience well and your exceptional ability to engage our leaders in apt discussions on a range of topics critical to their performance...has proven to be invaluable." *President, Vietnam Veterans of America*

"Bridget's listening, prompting, pushing, and cajoling in a way that brought out the best in every attendee, resulted in action plans that ensure that our organization tackles the important issues." *Executive Director, Connecticut Society of Association Executives*

"Ten hours with Bridget is better than 100 hours with my therapist!" *Client, Virginia*

"I wish to express my gratitude for all of the work and expertise you put into the presentation at our conference. You brought your A-game (I don't see you being able to bring anything else) and your energy to make our conference informative, entertaining and delightful to be at." *Seminar Participant, Chicago, IL*

"I had the pleasure of working with Bridget twice. After experiencing her facilitation of our complicated, executive management meeting I contacted her soon thereafter to run my team's "off-site." In Bridget's role as facilitator of the Executive Management meeting, she did a masterful job of getting the participants to agree on overall objectives and 'rules'. This served us well for the two days of discussions and set the framework for Bridget to keep the team away from the volatile, emotional side topics that would have derailed us and focused us on resolving the challenging problems in front of us. As the facilitator of my team's offsite, Bridget was a quick study in assessing each team member's strengths, weaknesses, and aspirations. In addition, she worked closely with me to set the meeting format and objectives, with the right amount of direction and guidance without forcing her perspective. Throughout the meeting, Bridget effectively led the team through the discussions and to a worthwhile conclusion, managing a wide array of personalities and handling each one in a way so that their input was obtained and overall buy in was achieved. Bridget is very insightful, approachable, and very helpful at bringing teams through difficult discussions to actionable conclusions." *VP of Product Management, Draeger Medical Systems*

"I really enjoyed and was inspired by your spirit and passion for getting those messages of hope to us. You filled our cup!" *Attendee, First Wednesdays.*

"The flower doesn't compare itself to other flowers.
It just blooms. Bloom." ~ Author Unknown

Made in the USA
Charleston, SC
19 April 2016